P9-API-738

Academic Language Mastery

Volumes in the
Academic Language Mastery Series

Series Editor: Ivannia Soto

Academic Language Mastery: Grammar and Syntax in Context
David E. Freeman, Yvonne S. Freeman, and Ivannia Soto

Academic Language Mastery: Conversational Discourse in Context
Jeff Zwiers and Ivannia Soto

Academic Language Mastery: Vocabulary in Context
Margarita Calderón and Ivannia Soto

Academic Language Mastery: Culture in Context
Noma LeMoine and Ivannia Soto

Academic Language Mastery:
Vocabulary
in Context

Margarita Calderón
Ivannia Soto

A SAGE Publishing Company

FOR INFORMATION:

Corwin

A SAGE Company

2455 Teller Road

Thousand Oaks, California 91320

(800) 233-9936

www.corwin.com

SAGE Publications Ltd.

1 Oliver's Yard

55 City Road

London EC1Y 1SP

United Kingdom

SAGE Publications India Pvt. Ltd.

B 1/I 1 Mohan Cooperative Industrial Area

Mathura Road, New Delhi 110 044

India

SAGE Publications Asia-Pacific Pte. Ltd.

3 Church Street

#10-04 Samsung Hub

Singapore 049483

Copyright © 2017 by Corwin

All rights reserved. When forms and sample documents are included, their use is authorized only by educators, local school sites, and/or noncommercial or nonprofit entities that have purchased the book. Except for that usage, no part of this book may be reproduced or utilized in any form or by any means, electronic or mechanical, including photocopying, recording, or by any information storage and retrieval system, without permission in writing from the publisher.

All trademarks depicted within this book, including trademarks appearing as part of a screenshot, figure, or other image, are included solely for the purpose of illustration and are the property of their respective holders. The use of the trademarks in no way indicates any relationship with, or endorsement by, the holders of said trademarks.

Printed in the United States of America

ISBN 978-1-5063-3807-1

This book is printed on acid-free paper.

Program Director: Dan Alpert

Senior Associate Editor: Kimberly Greenberg

Editorial Assistant: Katie Crilley

Production Editor: Amy Schroller

Copy Editor: Pam Schroeder

Typesetter: C&M Digitals (P) Ltd.

Proofreader: Dennis W. Webb

Indexer: Sheila Bodell

Cover Designer: Anupama Krishnan

Marketing Manager: Charline Maher

Certified Chain of Custody

SUSTAINABLE FORESTRY INITIATIVE

Promoting Sustainable Forestry

www.sfiprogram.org

SFI-01268

SFI label applies to text stock

16 17 18 19 20 10 9 8 7 6 5 4 3 2 1

DISCLAIMER: This book may direct you to access third-party content via Web links, QR codes, or other scannable technologies, which are provided for your reference by the author(s). Corwin makes no guarantee that such third-party content will be available for your use and encourages you to review the terms and conditions of such third-party content. Corwin takes no responsibility and assumes no liability for your use of any third-party content, nor does Corwin approve, sponsor, endorse, verify, or certify such third-party content.

Contents

Acknowledgments

I would like to acknowledge each of the authors who coauthored this series with me: Margarita Calderón, David and Yvonne Freeman, Noma LeMoine, and Jeff Zwiers. I have been inspired by each of your work for so long, and it was an honor learning and working with you on this project. I know that this book series is stronger due to each of your contributions, and will therefore affect the lives of so many English language learners (ELLs) and standard English learners (SELs). Thank you for taking this journey with me on behalf of students who need our collective voices!

I would also like to acknowledge my editor, Dan Alpert, who has believed in me and has supported my work since 2008. Thank you for tirelessly advocating for equity, including language equity, for so long! Thank you also for advocating for and believing in the vision of the Institute for Culturally and Linguistically Responsive Teaching (ICLRT)!

Also to be thanked is Corwin, for supporting my work over time as well as early contributions to ICLRT. Corwin has grown over the time that I published my first book in 2009, but they still remain a family. I would especially like to thank Michael Soule, Lisa Shaw, Kristin Anderson, Monique Corrdiori, Amelia Arias, Taryn Waters, Charline Maher, Kim Greenberg, and Katie Crilley for each of your parts in making this book series and ICLRT a success!

Last, I would like to acknowledge the California Community Foundation, whose two-year grant assisted greatly with fully launching ICLRT at Whittier College. Thank you for believing that effective professional development over time can and will create achievement and life changes for ELLs and SELs!

—Ivannia Soto, Series Editor

PUBLISHER'S ACKNOWLEDGMENTS

Corwin gratefully acknowledges the contributions of the following reviewers:

Bridget Erickson
Teacher, Literacy Specialist
Oakwood Elementary School
Wayzata Public Schools
Plymouth, MN

Gary Lee Frye
Development and Grant Coordinator
Lubbock-Cooper ISD
Lubbock, TX

Katherine Lobo
ESL Teacher, President of MATSOL
Newton South High School
Newton, MA

Valerie C. Ruff
Middle Grades Teacher
Druid Hills Academy
Charlotte, NC

Kerri Whipple
ELL Director
South East Education Cooperative
Fargo, ND

About the Authors

Dr. Margarita Calderón, is professor emerita senior research scientist at Johns Hopkins University School of Education. Since 2004, she has been conducting research studies funded by the Carnegie Corporation of New York. She has conducted longitudinal studies on English learners' language and literacy development in elementary, middle, and high schools and is now focusing on professional development designs for adopting evidence-based instruction.

The author of more than 100 articles, chapters, books, and teacher training manuals, Dr. Calderón's most recent professional book is *Teaching Reading to English Language Learners, Grades 6–12*. She also developed Reading Instructional Goals for Older Readers (RIGOR), a series of intervention resources for older students reading at preliterate through Grade 3 levels. RIGOR is being used in New York City, Boston, Houston, Louisville, Salt Lake City, and other major cities.

Dr. Calderón has worked as an English as a second language (ESL) high school teacher, a professional development coordinator for San Diego State University, and a bilingual director for the University of California at Santa Barbara. She presents frequently at conferences of major education organizations, including the International Reading Association, Teachers of English as a Second Language, and the National Association of Bilingual Educators.

Born in Juárez, Mexico, Dr. Calderón was educated in Mexico and the United States, receiving her BA in English and MA in linguistics from the University of Texas at El Paso, followed by a PhD from Claremont Graduate School in Pomona, California.

Dr. Ivannia Soto is associate professor of education at Whittier College, where she specializes in second language acquisition, systemic reform for ELLs and urban education. She began her career in the Los Angeles Unified School District (LAUSD), where she taught English and English language development to a population made up of 99.9 percent Latinos, who either were or had been ELLs. Before becoming a professor, Dr. Soto also served LAUSD as a literacy coach and district office administrator. She has presented on literacy and language topics at various conferences, including the National Association for Bilingual Education (NABE), the California Association for Bilingual Education (CABE), the American Educational Research Association (AERA), and the National Urban Education Conference. As a consultant, Soto has worked with Stanford University's School Redesign Network (SRN) and WestEd as well as a variety of districts and county offices in California, providing technical assistance for systemic reform for ELLs and Title III. Soto is the coauthor of *The Literacy Gaps: Building Bridges for ELLs and SELs* as well as author of *ELL Shadowing as a Catalyst for Change* and *From Spoken to Written Language with ELLs*, all published by Corwin. Together, the books tell a story of how to systemically close achievement gaps with ELLs by increasing their oral language production in academic areas. Soto is executive director of the Institute for Culturally and Linguistically Responsive Teaching (ICLRT) at Whittier College, whose mission it is to promote relevant research and develop academic resources for ELLs and Standard English Learners (SELs) via linguistically and culturally responsive teaching practices.

Series Dedication

I dedicate this book series to the teachers and administrators in Whittier Union High School District (WUHSD). WUHSD has been a pivotal learning partner with ICLRT over the past four years. By embedding ICLRT Design Principles and academic language development (ALD) best practices into their teaching and professional development, they have fully embraced and worked tirelessly in classrooms to meet the needs of ELLs and SELs. Specifically, I would like to thank Superintendent Sandy Thorstenson, Assistant Superintendent Loring Davies, and ELL Director Lilia Torres-Cooper (my high school counselor and the person who initially brought me into WUHSD) as well as ALD Certification teachers Diana Banzet, Amy Cantrell, Carlos Contreras, Carmen Telles Fox, Nellie Garcia, Kristin Kowalsky, Kelsey McDonnell, Damian Torres, and Heather Vernon, who have committed themselves fully to this work. I would also like to thank Lori Eshilian, principal of Whittier High School (my high school alma mater), for being willing to do whatever it takes to meet the needs of all students, including partnering with ICLRT on several projects over the past few years. You were my first and best physical education teacher and have modeled effective collaboration since I was in high school!

—Ivannia Soto, Series Editor

Book Dedication

I dedicate this book to all the educators in California who implemented and contributed to our work over the years. This includes the County Offices of Education that implemented the Multidistrict Trainer of Trainers Institutes where we piloted promising practices for integrating language, literacy and content back in the 1980s! A special thanks to Riverside and San Bernardino County teachers who participated in my study of Coaching and Its Impact on Teachers and Students (1984). These preliminary efforts have led to further refinements and training of thousands of teachers and administrators throughout the country with great outcomes.

I also dedicate this book to my dear friend Dan Alpert who has always believed in my efforts and helps me put them to print.

—Margarita Calderón

CHAPTER ONE

Introduction to the Book Series

According to the Migration Policy Institute (2013), close to 5 million U.S. students, which represent 9 percent of public school enrollment, are English language learners (ELLs). Three-quarters of these 5 million students were born in the United States and are either the children or grandchildren of immigrants. In some large urban school districts such as Los Angeles, ELLs already comprise around 30 percent of the student population. These demographic trends, along with the rigorous content expectations of new content and language standards (e.g., CCSS, WIDA, ELPA21, etc.), require that educational systems become skilled at simultaneously scaffolding academic language and content for this growing group of students. For ELLs, academic language mastery is the key to accessing rigorous content. Now is a pivotal time in educational history to address both academic language and content simultaneously so that ELLs do not fall further behind in both areas while also becoming bored by methods that are cognitively banal and lead to disengagement.

Another group of students who have academic language needs, but are not formally identified as such, are standard English learners (SELs). SELs are students who speak languages that do not correspond to Standard American English language structure and grammar but incorporates English vocabulary. They include African American students who speak African American Language (AAL), sometimes referred to as African American English, and Mexican American–non-new-immigrant students who speak Mexican American Language (MxAL) or what is commonly referred to as "Chicano English." ELLs and SELS also need instructional assistance in the academic language necessary to be successful in school, college, and beyond. For both groups of students, academic language represents the pathway to full access in meeting the rigorous demands of the new standards.

PURPOSE OF THIS ACADEMIC LANGUAGE DEVELOPMENT BOOK SERIES

The purpose of this series is to assist educators in developing expertise in, and practical strategies for, addressing four key dimensions of academic language when working with ELLs and SELs. To systemically address the needs of ELLs and SELs, we educators must share a common understanding of academic language development (ALD). Wong-Fillmore (2013) defines academic language as "the language of texts. The forms of speech and written discourse that are linguistic resources educated people in our society can draw on. This is language that is capable of supporting complex thought, argumentation, literacy, successful learning; it is the language used in written and spoken communication in college and beyond" (p. 15). Given that we are preparing ELLs and SELs for college, career, and beyond, they should receive ample opportunities to learn and use academic language, both in spoken and written form (Soto, 2014). ELLs and SELs also must be provided with scaffolded access to cognitively and linguistically demanding content, which allows them to cultivate their complex thinking and argumentation.

All students can benefit from academic language development modeling, scaffolding, and practice, but ELLs and SELs need it to survive and thrive in school. ELLs have plenty of language assets in their primary language that we must leverage to grow their academic English, yet there is often a very clear language and literacy gap that must be closed as soon as ELLs enter school. Similarly, SELs come to school with a language variation that, to be built upon in the classroom setting, must first be understood. In reviewing the wide range of literature by experts in this field, most agree that the key elements of academic English language for ELLs and SELs include these four dimensions: academic vocabulary, syntax and grammar, discourse, and culturally responsive teaching.

We have therefore organized this book series around these four dimensions of academic English:

- Conversational Discourse—developing students' conversational skills as an avenue for fostering academic language and thinking in a discipline
- Academic Vocabulary—teaching high-frequency academic words and discipline-specific vocabulary across content areas
- Syntax and Grammar—teaching sophisticated and complex syntactical and grammatical structures in context
- Culturally Responsive Teaching—incorporating culture while addressing and teaching language, and honoring students' home cultures and communities

The focus on these four dimensions in this book series makes this a unique offering for educators. By building upon the cultural and linguistic similarities of ELLs and SELs, we embed strategies and instructional approaches about academic vocabulary, discourse, and grammar and syntax within culturally responsive teaching practices, to make them all accessible to teachers of diverse students. As the American poet and great thinker of modern Hispanic literature, Sabine Ulibarrí, noted, "Language is culture; it carries with it traditions, customs, the very life of a people. You cannot separate one from the other. To love one is to love the other; to hate one is to hate the other. If one wants to destroy a people, take away their language and their culture will soon disappear." Therefore, the heart of this book series is to integrate language and culture in a manner that has not been addressed with other books or book series on ALD.

ACADEMIC LANGUAGE DEVELOPMENT DIMENSIONS DEFINED AND CONNECTIONS TO THE BOOK SERIES

ALD is a pathway to equity. With new rigorous state standards and expectations, ALD is the scaffold that provides access for ELLs and

SELs, so that high academic expectations can be maintained and reached. The following matrix defines each dimension of ALD, and demonstrates the connection of that ALD dimension across the book series. For full proficiency in ALD, it is integral that each

ALD Dimension	Definition	Connections to the Book Series
Academic Discourse	Academic discourse is putting words and sentences (the other two dimensions) together to clearly communicate complex ideas. The essential components of academic discourse include: • Message organization and text structure • Voice and register • Density of words, sentences, and ideas • Clarity and coherence • Purpose, functions, and audience	As suggested in the definition, academic discourse involves the overlap of academic vocabulary (words), and many of the components also often associated with academic writing across genres (organization, text structure, purpose, and audience). This book addresses a specific form of discourse, conversational discourse, and the specific conversational skills that provide access to academic discourse.
Academic Vocabulary	Words are separate units of information; it is tempting to focus on them as "pieces of knowledge" to accumulate to show learning. Instead, words should be tools and materials for constructing more complete and complex messages. In this book series, we will focus on Tier 2 (high-frequency words that go across content areas) and Tier 3 (abstract or nuanced words that exist within a particular content area or discipline) academic vocabulary.	Academic vocabulary is associated with the density of words used in academic discourse, as well as the use of connectives and transitions used in grammar.

ALD Dimension	Definition	Connections to the Book Series
Grammar/ Syntax in Context	Academic language is characterized by technical vocabulary, lexical density, and abstraction. Academic genres have predictable components, cohesive texts, and language structures that include nominalizations, passives, and complex sentences.	ELLs and SELs need to engage in academic discourse in the classroom and develop academic vocabulary. These are essential building blocks for learning to read and write cohesive texts using academic genres and the language structures characteristic of academic language.
Culturally and Linguistically Responsive Practices	Culturally responsive pedagogy incorporates high-status, accurate cultural knowledge about different ethnic groups into all subjects and skills taught. It validates, facilitates, liberates, and empowers ethnically diverse students by simultaneously cultivating their cultural integrity, individual abilities, and academic success (Gay, 2000).	ELLs and SELs are more likely to acquire ALD when they are viewed from an asset model and when ALD is taught as associated with concepts that connect to their cultural knowledge. This book will address linguistic diversity, including variations of English.

(Definitions adapted from Academic Language Development Network (n.d.) *unless otherwise noted)*

dimension be addressed across disciplines—the dimensions should not be taught as either/or skills. Instead, each of the dimensions should be addressed throughout a course of study or unit. In that way, it is important to read the book series in its entirety, as an ongoing professional development growth tool (more on that later). The matrix also demonstrates the connections made between ALD dimensions, which will prove helpful as readers continue their study across the ALD book series.

Format for Each Book

At the beginning of each book is an introduction to the purpose of the book series, including the format of each book and their intersections. Additionally, connections between current ALD research and the specific dimension of ALD are included in an abbreviated literature review. In the middle of each book, the voice of the expert in the particular ALD dimension is incorporated with practical strategies and classroom examples. These chapters include how to move from theory to practice, classroom examples at elementary and secondary levels, and ways to assess the dimension. At the end of each book, a summary of major points and how to overcome related challenges are included along with the rationale for use of the Institute for Culturally and Linguistically Responsive Teaching (ICLRT) Design Principles as a bridge between ALD and content. Also included at the end of each book are additional professional development resources.

Additionally, each book in the series is organized in a similar manner for ease of use by the reader. Chapter 1 is the introduction to the series of books, and not an introduction for each individual book. Instead, Chapter 2 introduces each dimension of ALD with the specific research base for that book. The heart of each book in the series is in Chapter 3, where practical application to theory and classroom examples can be found. Chapter 4 addresses how each ALD dimension fosters literacy development. This volume includes an additional chapter, Chapter 5, which discusses vocabulary instruction during reading. In Chapter 6, how to assess the specific ALD dimension is discussed with checklists and rubrics to assist with formative assessment in this area. This volume also addresses teaching vocabulary after reading in Chapter 6. Last, Chapter 7 connects each volume with others in the series and details how the book series can best be used in a professional development setting. The epilogue revisits the vision for the series and provides a description of the relationship to the underlying principles of the ICLRT.

- Chapter 1—Introduction to the Book Series
- Chapter 2—Connecting the Research on Academic Vocabulary and Discourse
- Chapter 3—Practical Application to the Classroom: Selecting Words to Teach
- Chapter 4—Fostering Literacy With Vocabulary: Teaching Words

- Chapter 5—Vocabulary Instruction During Reading
- Chapter 6—Vocabulary Assessment and Teaching Vocabulary After Reading
- Chapter 7—Conclusions, Challenges, and Connections
- Epilogue: The Vision

HOW TO USE THE BOOK SERIES

While each book can stand alone, the book series was designed to be read together with colleagues and over time. As such, it is a professional development tool for educational communities, which can also be used for extended learning on ALD. Educators may choose to begin with any of the four key dimensions of ALD that interests them the most or with which they need the most assistance.

HOW TO USE REFLECT AND APPLY QUERIES

Embedded throughout this book series you will find queries that will ask you to reflect and apply new learning to your own practice. Please note that you may choose to use the queries in a variety of settings: with a book study buddy during PLC, grade-level, or department meetings. Each of the queries can be answered in a separate journal while one is reading the text, or as a group you may choose to reflect on only a few queries throughout a chapter. Please feel free to use as many or as few queries as are helpful to you, but we do encourage you to at least try a couple out for reflection as you read the book series.

Try it out by responding to the first query here.

REFLECT AND APPLY

What does the following Sabine Ulibarrí quote mean to you? How does it connect to your students?

"Language is culture; it carries with it traditions, customs, the very life of a people. You cannot separate one from the other. To love one is to love the other; to hate one is to hate the other. If one wants to destroy a people, take away their language and their culture will soon disappear."

BOOK SERIES CONNECTION TO VOCABULARY

As previously discussed, academic vocabulary is an essential dimension of ALD. Often, however, educators may feel overwhelmed with the vocabulary gap that ELLs and SELs come to school with. They may feel that there are just too many words to teach or that it will take too long to close the vocabulary gap.

Vocabulary, however, is the backbone of language, and vocabulary learning should be a lifelong process. Focusing on Tier 2 and Tier 3 words with ELLs and SELs will in essence level the language playing field for these groups of students. For example, a fluent English speaker possesses approximately a written English vocabulary of 10,000 to 100,000 words. ELLs diversely know a range of 2,000 to 7,000 English words upon their commencement of academic studies (Hadley, 1993). To close this gap, Tier 2 and 3 words must be taught explicitly and intentionally.

The vocabulary methods introduced in this book in the series provide a theoretical and practical framework for addressing ALD in a contextualized manner and across disciplines. This short (teachers are busy people) book builds teachers' knowledge and confidence with respect to the core Tier 2 and Tier 3 vocabulary strategies that can be used in lessons to extend spoken and written communication skills.

CHAPTER TWO

Connecting the Research on Academic Vocabulary and Discourse

> Teaching vocabulary is not an end in itself. It is only a precursor into reading, writing, and conducting rich discussions in every content area.

WHY IS VOCABULARY SO IMPORTANT?

A rich language repertoire for any student is key for college and career readiness. What is more exciting is the opportunity that some students have to develop rich oral and written discourse in two or more languages. As the world becomes more and more interested in mastering second and third languages, our schools do not have to lag behind countries where many languages are valued and spoken. We have the potential in the United States for a multilingual and biliterate population.

Our country has a great advantage in developing high levels of language and literacy in two or more languages either simultaneously from early childhood or in quality, structured immersion programs for older students. We have evidence-based approaches for both (Slavin, Madden, Calderón, Chamberlain, & Hennessy, 2011).

We have the technology. We have the willing participants and their parents. What we need is the willpower and the courage to implement such programs that stress the development of a rich and comprehensive repertoire of vocabulary for all academic subjects and occasions (Hiebert & Kamil, 2005).

A recent trip to China was a wake-up call in several ways. First, we saw how teacher-training institutions are investing in preparing their faculty for developing and using academic English but not the written-only English as it was taught in the past, not the English that will simply help students pass the TOEFEL to be accepted into U.S. universities, and not touristy English. On the contrary, they are focusing on the academic English that targets oracy and rich discourse. They want the English of business negotiations, scientific discussions, joint research investigations and publications, and instruction in their elementary and secondary schools.

Isn't this the type of English that we want to develop in our elementary, middle, and high schools? As more students from Asia and Europe are able to enter our top universities, isn't it time to prepare our own students to be just as competitive as those students are? Our English learners are already on their way.

Language is the instrument to achieve intellectual, social, and economic success. Language is the means to express our ideas, reflections, and thoughts in speech and writing. Language expresses the ways we think and learn. It mirrors our personality as we express ourselves and interpret our critical thinking and ideas about people and the world we live in and continuously encounter. Language is what we share to build community. The more languages that we speak, the more communities we share. The more words we own to navigate new situations, the better we survive within those situations.

At the most basic level, oral language means communicating with other people. But when we talk about academic oral language development across the curriculum, we do not mean just teaching students to speak as much as we mean improving their ability to communicate more effectively. At higher academic levels, effective speech and communication involve thinking, content knowledge, and skills development—which require a context for continuous practice and training in every subject in every classroom, particularly in secondary schools.

> In our work with schools, we define *academic language* as a combination of words, phrases, sentences, and strategies to participate in class discussions, to show evidence of understanding and express complex concepts in texts, and to express oneself in academic writing.

State standards emphasize the development and use of academic language and discourse. For example, the California English Language Development (ELD) Standards state:

> [A]ll students are expected to participate in sustained dialogue on a variety of topics and content areas: explain their thinking and build on others' ideas; construct arguments and justify their positions persuasively with sound evidence; and, effectively produce written and oral texts in a variety of informational and literary text types. (California State Board of Education, 2013, p. 9–10)

The Common Core State Standards (CCSS) mention the word "vocabulary" more than 200 times. The section of the CCSS on college and career readiness and anchor standards for listening and speaking, Grades 6 through 12 (National Governors Association Center for Best Practices, & Council of Chief State School Officers, 2010) address two anchor standards: (1) comprehension and collaboration and (2) presentation of knowledge and ideas. Each has subcategories defining what a student should understand and be able to do by the end of each grade. For the most part, these are general statements that focus on the following:

- Engaging effectively in collaborative discussions (one-on-one, in groups, and teacher led) with diverse partners on topics, texts, and issues, building on others' ideas and expressing their own clearly:
  - Recounting, describing, or summarizing key ideas or details from the text
  - Asking and answering questions about what a speaker says

- o Summarizing what a speaker says and acknowledging new information, modifying one's own views
- o Presenting an argument with claims and counterclaims

California's Critical Principles for Developing Language and Cognition in Academic Contexts require the following:

While advancing along the continuum of English language development levels, English learners at all levels engage in intellectually challenging literacy, disciplinary, and disciplinary literacy tasks. They use language in meaningful and relevant ways appropriate to grade level, content area, topic, purpose, audience, and text type in English language arts, mathematics, science, social studies, and the arts. Specifically, they use language to gain and exchange information and ideas in three communicative modes (collaborative, interpretive, and productive), and they apply knowledge of language to academic tasks via three cross-mode language processes (structuring cohesive texts, expanding and enriching ideas, and connecting and condensing ideas) using various linguistic resources. (California State Board of Education, 2013, p. 46)

REFLECT AND APPLY

What do the CCSS and CA ELD standards call for which we haven't focused on before?

How do our curriculum, student reading texts, and my own instructional strategies address the standards?

FROM VOCABULARY TO DISCOURSE

Vocabulary is the centerpiece of discourse. Discourse is the spoken, written, or visual way of communicating. Academic discourse is guided by the information a teacher presents, the texts students are reading, and the intellectually engaging interactions with peers—all of which entail summarizing verbally and in writing. Without classroom opportunities to read, discuss, and summarize orally and in writing, ELLs cannot progress in their academic English development.

Vocabulary instruction is guided by context—the audience, the text structures, the author's purpose, and the discipline or content area. It is the role of the teacher to select key vocabulary and discourse features that students will need for comprehending and making meaning within a variety of communicative contexts (Graves, 2006; Nagy, 2005). The way we talk and write about science is different from the way we communicate in both modes in math. Math problems are succinct, and the language is very precise. The language of science is *tentative* in the sense that scientists always *suggest* rather than *assert* an answer. New math now asks for three or four ways of solving a problem, which means that more connectors and transition words need to be used such as *on the other hand* or *similarly* to connect the comparisons or contrasts. History books, and social studies texts in general, tend to have longer sentences and move back and forth between present, past, and future tenses. Literature, on the other hand, has a little of all these syntactical features but also uses more metaphors, similes, foreshadowing, rhyme, rhythm, and other features that distinguish it from the other subject areas. Hence, key vocabulary guides comprehension, quality discussions, and cohesive compositions for each content area. Most important, it anchors knowledge about the subjects students are studying.

How Do We Begin to Address These Language Demands?

To address these verbal and written demands of ELLs and SELs, teachers need to create repeated opportunities for ELLs to be engaged in high-level technical oral language discourse in student teams, one-on-one, or whole-class discussions around thought-provoking texts and topics. The process of becoming proficient begins with teachers identifying the small units of language—the vocabulary—followed by modeling how to use those vocabulary units within oracy, reading comprehension, and writing.

Notwithstanding the significance of vocabulary, the activities throughout a lesson require that students be knowledgeable about the topic to reiterate what they learned; affirm their knowledge; analyze, summarize, or synthesize information; restate facts; provide conclusions; and provide points of view. These common skills across the content areas must be explicitly taught to ELLs and SELs. ELLs benefit greatly from additional guided practice, corrective feedback, and instructional sequences that are taught systematically (Crawford-Brooke, 2013). Two of the best ways to teach these skills are for the teacher to model the words to express that skill through a Think Aloud and for students to interact with peers using that approach (Short & Fitzsimmons, 2007). (See examples in Chapter 4.)

THINK ABOUT IT

Why is it important to pre-teach five or so words before each subject lesson and not just in language arts or ELD/ESL classes?

CHAPTER THREE

Practical Application in the Classroom

Selecting Words to Teach

I f we select at least five key words to pre-teach before each content lesson in Grades K–12 grades, students will be able to tackle that subject much easier. Students will be able to comprehend better as they read the text and/or participate in the class discussion, brainstorming, or reviews. When they start reading the classroom text, knowing these words will give them confidence to keep reading, even if their English is very limited.

> Words should be selected to teach before, during, and after reading.

The first step in selecting words to teach before, during, and after reading is to categorize them into three tiers. Beck, McKeown, & Kucan (2002) made the field aware of how vocabulary could be categorized into three tiers to encourage educators to teach vocabulary. Their teacher-friendly definition made great sense for teaching all students. Their work became part of the foundation of our ongoing research on academic language and literacy development. As we began to work with the three tiers through a 5-year study in 2005 funded by the Carnegie Corporation of New York, we found the tiers to be a powerful tool for teaching language to ELLs as a precursor to the development of reading and writing skills in each subject area. As we tested the tiers in elementary, middle, and high schools with ELLs and SELs in the same classrooms, modifications emerged (Calderón, 2007; Calderón, Carreón, Duran, & Fitch 2009). We called the professional development program for teaching academic language and vocabulary, reading comprehension, and writing Expediting Comprehension for English Language Learners™ (ExC-ELL™). With widespread implementation in Chinese, Haitian, and Spanish dual-language schools and in multiple language classrooms, modifications and recent additions shaped the most effective ways to teach vocabulary before, during, and after reading and for formal writing in Pre-K through 12th-grade classrooms (Calderón et al., 2015).

What Are Some Key Differences Between EL and Mainstream Tiers?

The seminal work of Beck and colleagues (2002, 2005) offered this definition of the three vocabulary tiers:

> The first tier consists of the most basic words—*clock, baby, happy, walk,* and so on. Words in this tier rarely require instructional attention to their meanings in school. The third tier is made up of words whose frequency of use is quite low and often limited to specific domains . . . *isotope, lathe, peninsula,* and *refinery.* The second tier contains words that are of high frequency for mature language users and are found across a variety of domains. Examples include *coincidence, absurd, industrious,* and *fortunate.* Instruction directed toward Tier 2 words can be most productive.

Beck et al. (2002) estimate that there are 8,000 Tier 1 word families. Families are groups of related words such as *introduce, introduction, reintroduce,* and *introducing,* and the authors state that these "need no instruction." However, for ELLs, we find that these families and even simpler Tier 1 word families such as *walk, walking, walked, walk-through, walk off,* and *walk away* do need instruction. Many of these words that appear to be Tier 1 are actually quite difficult for ELLs because they have multiple meanings such as the word *trunk* (*tree trunk, car trunk, chest, torso,* and *elephant trunk*) or appear in certain idioms or collocations (*trunk show*, *trunk line*, and *swimming trunks*). Hence, when selecting words to teach to ELLs, it is important for teachers to consider which Tier 1 words also need to be taught.

When it comes to Tier 2 words, Beck and colleagues (2002) found about 7,000 and recommend that an average of 700 Tier 2 words be taught per year. This is of course a recommendation for mainstream students. However, Biemiller (2011) found that by the end of 12th grade, students should have a verbal command of 50,000 words. That means that ELLs should learn 3,000 to 5,000 words per year to catch up with mainstream students. Of course, this should be a combination of Tier 1, 2, and 3 words. Because there are so many words to teach, the explicit teaching should concentrate on Tier 2. After years of testing various components, we have found the most efficient way to select words to pre-teach at the beginning of each class. A second set can be taught "on the run" and a third set as a word-study activity in centers, for homework, before writing a composition, or as a sponge activity. A sponge activity is one that teachers use "to soak up the time" before the bell rings or when students finish a task and need more to do.

FIVE THOUSAND WORDS A YEAR!

Biemiller (2011) recommends that students learn between the 3,000 and 5,000 words per year to know at least 50,000 words by high school graduation. Hence, if all teachers *in all grade levels* in a school pre-teach five words per subject per day before reading, that equals 25 words a day. Twenty-five words times 5 days a week equals 125. One hundred and twenty-five words times 30 weeks (could be more) equals 3,750 words a year. They learn others as they read. Vocabulary should be a precursor to reading.

WHAT ARE SOME EXAMPLES OF THE THREE TIERS FOR ELLS?

Working with ELL specialists and core content teachers has helped solidify consistent success with ELLs, SELs, striving readers, and general education students with the following framework. Although there is sometimes a blurred line between categories and subcategories, this framework has helped educators (1) select key words to teach ELLs based on a three-tier framework specifically developed for ELLs; (2) teach the vocabulary tiers, particularly Tier 2 and 3; and (3) integrate vocabulary instruction into oral discourse, reading, and writing in the content areas to ensure students master content along with the development of language and literacy (Calderón, 2007, 2011).

English learners (ELs) and SELs often struggle to comprehend and learn core content concepts due to insufficient academic vocabulary. Academic language begins with selecting vocabulary, having students apply words in the four domains. They need rich and varied language experiences in four domains:

Speaking—responding to questions, asking questions, discussions, and oral summaries using Tier 2 and 3 words that were pre-taught

Listening—to teachers and peers use academic language, television, computer programs, and repeating using as many Tier 2 and 3 words as possible

Reading—read alouds, peer reading, and independent reading while applying new vocabulary

Writing—summaries, text-based writing, research papers using as many Tier 2 and 3 words and phrases as possible

Whereas each subject area has its own Tier 3 words, they share many of the Tier 2 words. Yet the Tier 2 words have subtle or not-so-subtle changes across subject areas and therefore cause many comprehension problems (e.g., *dining table, table of contents, multiplication table, chemistry table, water table, table the decision* or *discussion, table food, table license, table mat,* and *table manners*).

REFLECT AND APPLY

How many words are your ELLs and SELs learning per year? How about in every content area?

How many are they reading and writing?

OVERVIEW OF TIER 3, TIER 2, AND TIER 1 WORDS AND PHRASES

All three tiers of words and phrases are critical to understanding science, math, social studies, language arts, computers, fine arts, physical education, and any other subject matter. The examples in this chapter are excerpts from our Expediting Comprehension for English Language Learners™ (ExC-ELL™) study and the professional development manuals that were developed from the Carnegie Corporation of New York and the U.S. Department of Education studies (Calderón, Carreón, Slakk, Trejo, & Peyton, 2010–2016).

Tier 3 Words

Tier 3 words are subject-specific words. They are sometimes called technical words. These are the words that convey concepts relevant to the topics being studied (e.g., in science: *protons, matter,* and *chemical reaction*). They represent the main concepts in the topic or theme discussed in the text and are often highlighted in textbooks and defined in the glossary. As can be seen in curriculum frameworks, these words are an important component for learning the subject and are typically found in state-related tests.

Many concepts come in phrases: *chemical reaction, ice ages, fractal geometry, North Pole,* and *even numbers.* When it comes to teaching concepts, we can also cluster them into phrases for ease of teaching, for example: *chaotic phenomena, greenhouse gas emissions, climate change,* and *counterarguments.*

It is important to select Tier 3 words that are key to understanding the concept and to make sure students use these words throughout the lesson to master the concept. However, most Tier 3 words cannot be taught before students read them in context, particularly words and phrases in science such as *photosynthesis* or *greenhouse gas emissions.* Unless conducting an experiment, it would take too much time to try to teach *photosynthesis* if the students do not gather all the valuable related information from a text. The text usually defines the word in the sentence where it is found, is accompanied by illustrations, and provides additional background knowledge necessary to understand the concept. In cases such as these, it is better to identify these Tier 3 words, post them where students can see them, but tell them that they will be reading to understand the whole concept. After reading, they will discuss and participate in other activities to reinforce their meaning. (How to teach words before, during, and after reading is discussed in subsequent chapters.)

In Elementary Schools:
Tier 3 Vocabulary Instruction

Pre-K to 5th-grade teachers have more opportunities to teach 25 words a day. They can pre-teach five words for math, five for science, five for language arts, five for social studies, and five for electives or transition times or other daily activities. There are quick vocabulary activities for after reading or for pairs or individual students to do in centers. The most important thing to remember is that students need to read these 25 words in context. If textbooks are not available for science or social studies, theme-based texts can be downloaded from the Internet at all grade levels (e.g., READWORKS, see http://www.readworks.org/books/passages?gclid=CJqYj93Iscw CFcUmhgodw7IJng). The writing that K through 5th-grade students do on a daily basis should be based on the mentor text they have been reading, and they should include as many Tier 2 and Tier 3 words as possible. Some teachers grade student writing based on the number of Tier 2 and 3 words that are used correctly.

In Secondary Schools:
Tier 3 Vocabulary Instruction in Science

In secondary schools, ELLs have double the work in learning because they have to master both content and the language of that content (Short & Fitzsimmons, 2007). Some students in secondary schools do not master the key vocabulary and sentence combinations that embody important science concepts such as *energy, photosynthesis,* or *osmosis* because these Tier 3 words are found in sentences that have unfamiliar Tier 2 words and phrases—maybe even some Tier 1 words as well. Speaking, reading, and writing about science largely hinges on the reader and writer's ability to make clear connections among scientific assertions, processes, and tentative statements. The tentativeness of science is reflected through words and phrases such as *it is suggested, notwithstanding,* and *albeit*. Additionally, almost every sentence needs to rely on the previous sentence and contributes to the next. This logic-based linking of concepts and expression is what ultimately guides the reader from one idea to the next.

The fact that Tier 3 words are usually nested in long sentences becomes a huge challenge for ELs. Those sentences contain many other words that are also unfamiliar to them.

> It is often those "little words or phrases," such as *so that, over the course of,* and *nonetheless* that can make a concept incomprehensible, whether it is spoken or written.

In writing about science, syntactic constructions explain the relationships between a student having understood the text and interpretations of the scientific processes and concepts in that text. These tentative words, connectors, or clusters are key for this logic-based thinking (e.g., A growing number of studies <u>suggest, however</u>, that *such an increase could have* a big <u>*impact*</u> on life). These transition words and phrases are part of the Tier 2 category of words. Therefore, explicit instruction on Tier 2 words and clusters needs as much emphasis as that of Tier 3 science-specific words, or those in social studies and math, as well as those found in literature and language arts.

Tier 2 and some Tier 3 words and phrases will require pre-teaching before students are exposed to an experience or experiment with science. Some inquiry methods in science call for an experience that demonstrates the key concepts for that unit of instruction before labeling the concepts. The labels for those concepts would of course be Tier 3 words. However, without pre-teaching some key science terms, connectors, transition words, and polysemous words, students could miss out on understanding 80 percent or more of the experiment or experience! Unless students know 80 to 90 percent of the words in a sentence or an explanation (even with visuals and hands-on tools), we cannot ensure comprehension of that experience. Selected words can be taught during an experience by simply showing the item or doing the motion while saying the word and having students repeat it three times, turn to their partner, and use the word in the same sentence the teacher used. This is a quick way of helping students begin to anchor the vocabulary. Some teachers prefer to pre-teach four or five key words or phrases using the seven-step method; then they teach others during the experience also using the seven steps or the "repeat what I just said to your buddy" method. Unless students also read a text or texts, summarize what they observed, and read and write about that experience, the connections among listening, speaking, reading, and writing are lost.

REFLECT AND APPLY

Although we spend most of our instructional time teaching Tier 3 words, think of a time when your students missed a test question or were thrown off by a simple word such as "state why the State of New York" (leaving the student perplexed) or phrase such as "draw a conclusion" (where the student draws instead of writes).

What examples can you think of?

How did the Tier 2 word(s) confuse the student?

Tier 2 Words and Subcategories

The Tier 2 category includes multiple types of words and phrases. The concepts that Tier 3 represent are nested in Tier 2 words in texts and in the teacher's presentations, explanations, and experiments. Even if students understand all of the Tier 3 words in a text or experiment, failure to know the supporting Tier 2 words and phrases will inhibit their ability to fully comprehend the concepts represented by Tier 3 words.

We find that teachers like to cluster Tier 2 words under several subcategories to help remember the types of words they might want to choose to pre-teach and which they can teach later on as students read or before they write about what they read. There is no right or wrong way to cluster words and phrases. This is one approach:

Tier 2 Subcategories

- Transition Words
- Phrases and Clusters
- Polysemous Words (Homonyms or Homographs)

- Cognates and False Cognates
- More Sophisticated Words for Rich Discussions and for Specificity
- Idioms and Collocations

(Examples to follow from Calderón et al., 2010–2016)

Transition and Connectors

Transition words or phrases are used to connect ideas, to help the reader progress from one idea to the next, and to show the relationship between a main idea and supporting details. Transition words and phrases may express sequence and chronology, causation, addition, concession, contradiction, temporal, and other relationships.

The following clusters are some examples of frequently used transition words we have collected from the K–12 teachers we work with. They report that these are the words that make a huge difference in accelerating spoken and written language. All students benefit from learning and using these words on a daily basis. Even kindergarten children love to use words such as *moreover*!

- ***Transitions to Express Sequence and Chronology:*** after, afterward, again, as long as, at last, at length, at that time, at that moment, at the same time, at this point, at this time
- ***Temporal Transition Words or Phrases.*** Indicating transitions across time and calendar, for example: the day before yesterday, last night, two weeks ago, today, at this moment, over the course of, next week, week after next, in a little while, in a few minutes
- ***Transitions to Express Causation:*** accordingly, after all, as, because of this, by this means, consequently, for this reason, hence, in course, then, therefore, thus, to be sure
- ***Transitions to Express Effect:*** as a result, because, thus, in consequence, as a consequence, so that, for this reason, accordingly, therefore
- ***Transitions to Express Addition:*** additionally, again, also, and, and then, as well, besides, equally important, finally, first (second, third, etc.), further, furthermore, in addition
- ***Transitions to Express Concession:*** although it is true that, certainly, despite this, granted that, however, indeed, granted, I admit that, in fact, in spite of, it may appear that

- *Transitions to Express Contradiction:* although, but, contra-dicting, despite (the fact that), however, in contrast, in spite of the fact that, in spite of this

Source: Calderón & Slakk, Teaching Vocabulary. Indianapolis, IN: Solution Tree; see Gregory M. Campbell (1994) for similar and comprehensive lists by categories.

Phrases and Clusters

The Tier 2 transition phrases and other clusters need to be taught as one word or one unit of meaning the same way we teach idioms. This also saves the teachers time and effort by not sepa-rating the words in the phrases and helps students remember how to use them (see the example of how to teach them in the next chapter). Examples of frequently used phrases and clusters include the following:

Over the course of . . .

The previous does not imply . . .

I concur with that idea because . . .

I respectfully disagree because . . .

However, on page . . . it states . . .

One piece of evidence is on page . . .

Teaching phrases helps ELs and SELs connect ideas by com-bining clauses in a wide variety of ways as stated by the California English language development (ELD) standards:

(e.g., creating compound and complex sentences) to make connections between and join ideas, for example, to express cause/effect (e.g., The deer ran *because* the mountain lion approached them), to make a concession (e.g., She studied all night *even though* she wasn't feeling well), or to link two ideas that happen at the same time (e.g., The cubs played *while* their mother hunted). (California State Board of Education, 2013, p. 63).

Polysemous Words

Polysemous words have multiple meanings. They range from completely unrelated words such as an *elephant trunk* and a *car trunk* to those that are subtler in meaning such as *divide*: *He divided up the rest of the money. Tier 2 words can be divided into different subcategories. The trust was divided among the relatives.*

Here are some more frequently used examples of words that appear to be "easy Tier 1" words but have up to 50 different meanings when we consider them in word families (e.g., *power, powered, powerful, powering, powerless,* and *powers*) or collocations or idioms (e.g., *the powers that be, the power of speech,* and *generating power*).

Polysemous words can be either Tier 3, 2, or 1. The following examples of Tier 3 words can be used in math, science, social studies, or language arts with subtle differences:

divide	density	solution	radical
prism	degree	image	radian

REFLECT AND APPLY

Can you think of other polysemous words? Look at the texts you currently use, and find as many polysemous words as possible.

Cognates

ELs who speak a Romance language (particularly Spanish, French, Italian, or Portuguese) and have literacy experiences in their primary language have a great advantage when it comes to learning science, math, and social studies in English. The reason is that more than 40 percent of the technical terms or key vocabulary in English has cognates in those languages. These may be Tier 3 or Tier 2 words. Many words that are Tier 1 in Spanish, for example, are Tier 2 in English (e.g., facil/facile and edificio/edifice. The following are common words used in all content areas.

Common Information-Processing Words	Spanish Cognate
analyze	analizar
apply	aplicar
classify	clasificar
clarify	clarificar
communicate	comunicar
compare	comparar
contrast	contrastar
conclude	concluir

False Cognates

The standards also call for pointing out similarities and differences between the native language and English for potential transference. Sometimes the transference can lead to interference. For instance, false cognates can confuse students. Words such as *character* does not mean *carácter* (personality). *Exit* does not mean *éxito* (success), and *suceso* in Spanish means *event* in English. There are several cognates and false cognates dictionaries one can find on the Internet that can be easily consulted. Online resources such as the following also exist: http:// www.realfastspanish.com/vocabulary/spanish-cognates.

Words for Specificity

Tier 1 words that students use often (e.g., *say/said* and *but*) can be replaced with more sophisticated Tier 2 words. For example, students might replace *say/said* with any of these words depending on the meaning that they want to convey: *announce, articulate, comment, describe, discuss, mention, question, remark, specify,* or *verbalize*. All of these sophisticated words have cognates in Spanish.

Some English-Spanish Words That Can Replace Tier 1 *Say/Said*	
announce *anunciar*	mention *mencionar*
articulate *articular*	question *cuestionar*
comment *comentar*	remark *remarcar*
describe *describir*	specify *especificar*
discuss *discutir*	verbalize *verbalizar*

Collocations

Collocations are a pair or group of words that are habitually juxtaposed in a typical English manner. We don't typically say the America flag is white, blue, and red. We always say red, white and blue. We say PB&J (peanut butter and jelly) not J&PB. Other examples include the following:

safe and sound (Spanish speakers' collocation is *sano y salvo*)

true or false

yes or no

salt and pepper

Idioms

The Cambridge dictionary defines an *idiom* as a group of words whose meaning is considered as a unit is different from the meaning of each word considered separately. Idioms are particular to a group of people:

Down to earth, from the horse's mouth, break a leg, lend a hand, shoot yourself in the foot, hand over foot, lend me your ear, the early bird, break the bank, sing all the way to the bank, she's out in left field, she's rolling in money, small talk, talk a mile a minute, dance around a topic, hit a brick wall, talk back

REFLECT AND APPLY

Which of the Tier 2 subcategories do you typically teach? Which need more attention?

Tier 1 Words

Tier 1 words are everyday words. They are usually basic words that are known by most students in an age group or grade. However, ELs may not necessarily know them. Their unfamiliarity of Tier 1 words may be a result of a lack of background knowledge to understand the word or awareness of spelling, decoding, pronunciation, grammar, or co-location in English. Although Tier 1 words are the easiest words in a text, they are the most difficult to identify for instruction because the teacher may not know ahead of time which ones a particular student knows or needs to know. Nonetheless, they are equally important for a teacher to intentionally teach.

ELLs who enter the English language learning process later, whether they be students with interrupted formal education (SIFE) or are simply newcomers at a later point in life also need these Tier 1 words explicitly taught. ELLs with special educational needs may equally fall into this category of explicitly needed instruction.

A teacher should begin by selecting those Tier 1 words that they have noticed the students have not yet acquired. As the teacher begins to know the students' abilities, they should modify the list of Tier 1 words that specific students need. A teacher can collect informal data by watching and listening to students as they interact, read, and write. Tier 1 words include those that present the following challenges: spelling (e.g., *tough* or *toothache*), pronunciation (e.g., *ship/chip* or *very/berry*), limited background knowledge (e.g., *blender* and *lawnmower*), and possible false cognates (e.g., exit/*éxito*, which means "success" in Spanish). From Calderón et al., 2005; Calderón, 2007, 2011; Calderón et al., 2010–2016.

This identification process applies to all grade levels. Early childhood trade books and reading textbooks usually have more Tier 1 words (sight words and low-frequency words) than upper grade texts. Nevertheless, typical trade books also have some Tier 2 phrases and a lot of idioms that need to be taught. As I observed one first-grade classroom, I saw Miguelito sitting in the front row on the rug as his teacher read a story. He kept making strange faces throughout the reading. Afterward, I called him over and asked why he was making those faces. He said, "My teacher, she is crazy, she say elephants have square trunk full of gold. Elephants have long trunk." I immediately figured that his mind movie was seeing an elephant, whereas the trunk in the story referred to a chest full of gold. He totally missed the story line. Not just from not knowing the other meaning of trunk but for remaining perplexed trying to figure out what the elephant had to do with the rest of the story.

Sample Chart to Post in the Classroom

Teachers use a chart similar to this one to categorize the words. Subsequently, they post it on large chart paper and keep it posted throughout the lesson so that students can use the words during writing and discussions and to become vicariously familiar with the tiers. Begin by finding Tier 3. Go back and find Tier 2. Finally, thinking about your students at Levels 1 and 2 (emerging) proficiency, try to identify three or four Tier 1 words that you know they need to learn and apply.

Word Categories Chart

Type of Words	Tier 3	Tier 2	Tier 1
Polysemous			
Homophones			
Phrasal clusters, idioms			
Information processing			
Connectors and transitions			
Cognates			
False cognates			
Other			

Source: Calderón et al. (2010–2016).

REFLECT AND APPLY

Reread the text your students will use next week. Use the chart to categorize Tier 3, 2, and 1 words you find in that text. Select the five you deem most critical for your students' understanding of that text.

CHAPTER FOUR

Fostering Literacy With Vocabulary

Teaching Words

Select words to teach before reading, during reading, and after reading to build redundancy and mastery.

Teachers select vocabulary to teach from the texts students will read, from experiments to conduct, or from the language the teacher will use for explanations. They select words and phrases that they believe ELLs need (1) to know to comprehend the text, (2) to discuss those concepts, and (3) to use in their writing later on. After making the list and categorizing words, the next step is to select some to pre-teach before students read or listen to content-specific delivery.

Five or six words should be selected for pre-teaching. More words can be taught during and after reading and before writing. Initially, a teacher will probably end up with a long list of words for each tier. However, the list can be considerably reduced using the following checklist.

CRITERIA FOR SELECTING WORDS TO TEACH

- Words and phrases you want to hear in their discussions
- Words and phrases that are important and useful for understanding the text, the concept, and the knowledge to master
- Words, phrases, and sentence structures that have instructional potential for enhancing reading and writing skills and language learning in all subjects
- Words, phrases, and sentence structures you want to see in the students' short and long pieces of writing
- Words and phrases that are found in critical tests

Source: Calderón et al. (2010–2016).

Once the words have been meticulously selected, the five that will facilitate better understanding of the text will be the ones to pre-teach. Most of those five words will probably be Tier 2 words or phrases. Others can be set aside to teach throughout the course of the lesson. As students read, additional words will most likely be found that need attention. In diverse and mixed-ability classes, all students will benefit from instruction on different types of words. All students need specificity of definitions and more practice using them with precision, particularly in their writing.

WHY EMPHASIZE TIER 2 MORE THAN TIER 3 VOCABULARY?

As mentioned previously, Tier 3 vocabulary is presented and empha-sized recurrently, often redundantly, in lessons and textbooks. Tier 3 words typically appear many times in an explanation, experience, or experiment. In a text, not only is the word defined in the sentence, but it is often also portrayed through pictures, diagrams, drawings, sche-matics, tables, and other visuals. It is also defined in the glossary. However, most textbooks do not highlight the Tier 2 words or repre-sent them in repetitive ways. Hence, Tier 2 vocabulary must be taught explicitly through a seven-step process that only takes 2 or 3 minutes per word or phrase (Calderón, 2007; Calderón et al., 2005, 2015). Of course, some Tier 3 and even Tier 1 words can be taught with the following seven-step process if necessary.

Here is an example from a narrative text on how to select words and phrases that are important to ELs from *Chato's Kitchen* by Gary Soto and Susan Guevara (1995).

Yes, it was a whole family of fat, juicy mice moving into the house next door. Chato raked his tongue over his lips and meowed a deep growling meow. The mice froze with their belongings on their backs. They began to shiver like leaves in the wind. Chato was the tallest cat they had ever seen!

Tier 1—words that can be taught on the run	Tier 2—words or phrases of high value for ELs that should be taught using the seven steps	Tier 3—subject or topic specific
raked	whole family	Chato
growling	belongings	
shiver	had ever seen	
meowed		
mice froze		

The Tier 1 words can usually be quickly explained with gestures, movement, sounds, or pictures. The Tier 2 words or phrases need more instruction as described in the seven steps to follow. We select "whole family," which may seem simple enough, but what does "whole" mean in this context? "Belongings" used as a plural noun is quite different from the verb "belong," and "had ever seen" as the past participle is a common phrase that has high utility for ELs because they can use it in other classes or other occasions.

Thus, we select words that are of high utility for ELs. If books highlight words such as *yarn* and *dye*, words that ELs might never have to use again, it is better to select others that will be useful. The following is an example for upper-grade social studies:

Political Reasons for Migration

People may migrate because they are not happy with the political *structures*, leadership, or decisions in their home country. Not many people *realize* that after the American Civil War (1861–1865), approximately 20,000 former *supporters* of the Confederate *cause* (southern states that *supported* slavery) *emigrated* to Brazil, where slavery was still legal. Some of the *emigrees* returned to the United States, and others became Brazilian citizens.

Source: Human Migration and Global Change by Joy Peyton (2014).

Tier 1—words that can be taught on the run	Tier 2—words or phrases of high value for ELs that should be taught using the seven steps	Tier 3—subject or topic specific
may	decisions	migrate
home country	realize	political structures
	approximately	Confederate cause
	former supporters	southern states
		slavery
		emigrees

For the upper grades, there will still be Tier 1 words that might be troublesome for some ELs or those that need specificity in meaning, such as "may" and "home country." There will be more Tier 2 words such as those on the chart that nest the concepts that the Tier 3 words are attempting to convey. Tier 2 words are the ones to teach through the seven-step method. Tier 3 words are loaded with background history (e.g., "slavery" and "southern states") that ELs may not have. Therefore, it is important to give a little background by using the seven steps for some of these as well. More examples follow after the explanation of the seven-step process.

Seven-Step Process for Pre-Teaching Vocabulary in Grades 2 Through 12

---

1. Teacher says the word (or phrase). Then the teacher asks students to repeat it three times.

2. Teacher states the word in context—states the sentence where it is found in the text or from a teacher's explanation.

3. Teacher provides a dictionary definition(s).

4. Teacher explains the meaning with student-friendly definitions or examples.

5. Teacher highlights one trait of the word or phrase: grammatical aspect, spelling, polysemy, cognate, and so on.

6. *Teacher asks students to practice using the word in five or more sentences, each with a partner to anchor the word and concept knowledge.*

7. Teacher reminds the students how they will be held accountable for using the word (e.g., in peer summaries, exit passes, or other writing assignments).

Sources: Calderón (2007); Calderón et al. (2011–2016).

All seven steps are laid out on a PowerPoint slide or on chart paper when presented to the students. The teacher's Steps 1 to 5 should only take 1 minute or perhaps 2 minutes in the first few trials with this strategy. This is teacher time. Do not ask students to guess what the meaning is or who has heard this word before or such questions. This will only distract the students from your brisk but effective explanation by taking up precious time.

For *Step 1* students need to repeat the word at least three times after the teacher to become familiar with its pronunciation. Teachers like to add creativity to this step. A teacher will ask students to repeat the word three times after her or him and, following that, to whisper the word three more times to their buddies. This helps them become comfortable with the word before they use it in sentences during Step 6.

Step 2 is for the teacher to present the word in the sentence exactly as it appears in the text they are about to read. This helps students familiarize themselves further with how the word will be used in this lesson.

Step 3 provides the dictionary definition the teacher has selected. We don't want to send the students to look up the word in the dictionary because that will take up too much time. Furthermore, if it is a polysemous word; they are likely to select the wrong meaning.

Step 4 is an opportunity to clarify the dictionary definition by using student-friendly explanations, examples, or pictures that go with the explanation.

Step 5 is an opportunity for the teacher to add something, *very quickly*, about the syntactical aspect of the word. Is it in the past tense? Plural form? Is it a connector or prepositional phrase? Does it bring two short sentences together? Is it a cognate or false cognate? Does it contain a prefix or suffix, and what can these tell us? This may also be where the teacher explains that in a different class, the word may be used in a different manner, but for the purposes of this lesson, to use the given definition.

Step 6 gives students the first opportunity to use the word in a meaningful sentence. Each student should practice with *one student only* using the word in a few sentences each, back and forth, for 1 minute. Be sure to time them, and let them know when the minute is up. Use sentence frames where they have to use the word to help students ease into conversation and for coming up with good examples.

Step 7 is for the teacher to point out in a few seconds how they have to use the word in follow-up activities once you have pre-taught all five words. With Step 7 you are holding them accountable for using academic language in oral and written tasks that day. With this, students will readily understand that the onus is on them to master the words as they continue to use them 30 or more times in the lesson's sequence of learning activities.

The seven-step strategy is typically used in Grades 2 through 12 and for university students. The five dual-language universities Ana G. Mendéz, in Florida, DC, and Texas, are also using the seven-step strategy in Spanish and English for their graduate and undergraduate students who are enrolled in their business, criminal justice, nursing, and teacher education departments. The university system wants their graduates to be fully bilingual and biliterate in Spanish and English. The seven steps for second grade through the university level come together as illustrated in this example:

(1) Teacher: Say *notwithstanding* three times after I say each word.

(2) Students: *Notwithstanding, notwithstanding, notwithstanding.*

(3) Teacher: Now, turn to your elbow buddy and both whisper *notwithstanding* three more times.

(4) Students (whispering):   *Notwithstanding, notwithstanding, notwithstanding.*

(3) Teacher: You will find the word *notwithstanding* in this sentence: *Notwithstanding* the evidence, the jury did not reach a verdict.

(4) Teacher: The dictionary definition that fits our meaning for today is: *in spite of.*

(5) Teacher: We can use *although* and say: *Although* the jury had a lot of evidence against this person, they did not decide if he was guilty or not.

(6) Teacher: *Notwithstanding* is a preposition like the word *although*. Later we will see how it can also be used as an adverb or a conjunction.

(7) Teacher: Turn to your buddy and give each other at least five examples on how to use the word. Use this frame for your examples: *Notwithstanding* the (difficult test, terrible wind, rain, etc.) I survived. You have 1 minute. If some of you run out of ideas, repeat what your buddy said. I will be monitoring to listen for *notwithstanding*.

(8) Students: "*Notwithstanding* the snow last week, I survived." (Twenty-four students, sitting in pairs, provide anywhere from three to five examples. each taking turns.)

(9) Teacher: One minute is up. Be sure to use *notwithstanding* in your exit pass at the end of the day and in your essay due Friday.

PRE-TEACHING WORDS IN
PRE-K–1ST GRADE OR FOR NEWCOMERS

The five-step process is for the early grades, Pre-K through first grade, or for recent newcomers. The dictionary definition and the grammar explanation can be left out to get quickly to the student practice. Here is an example for Pre-K to first grades and/or newcomers in the upper grades:

(1)	Teacher:	Say *I'm sorry* three times after I say it.
(2)	Students:	*I'm sorry, I'm sorry, I'm sorry.*
(3)	Teacher:	Now turn to your other buddy on the left, say *I'm sorry* three times, and pretend you are crying.
(4)	Students (rubbing their eyes and pretending to cry):	*I'm sorry, I'm sorry, I'm sorry!*
(5)	Teacher:	The title of our story today is "I'm Sorry." We are going to read to find out who is sorry and why.
(6)	Teacher:	You say *I'm sorry* when you do something bad accidently. For example, I stepped on Tony's foot, and I said, "I'm sorry I stepped on your foot." Pablo forgot his homework, and he said, "Teacher, I'm sorry I forgot my homework."
(7)	Teacher:	Now take turns and tell your partner: *I am sorry I* _____. I will time you and let you know when the minute is up.
(8)	Students:	(All give each other several examples.)
(9)	Teacher:	Who wants to tell me what your buddy said? Three volunteers, please?

(10)   Three students: (1) My buddy said he is sorry he broke my pencil. (2) My buddy said she is sorry she ate my candy. (3) My buddy said she is sorry she forgot the answer!

(11)   Teacher: Remember, it is nice to say *I'm sorry* when you do something bad, something wrong, or something you did not mean to do. Let's read about Sheryl and why she was sorry. Please use *sorry* when you summarize with your buddy.

After teaching one word with the five or seven steps, teachers continue teaching three or four more. Here are some things to avoid when pre-teaching the words:

UNINTENDED AND INAPPROPRIATE WAYS TO APPROACH VOCABULARY INSTRUCTION

When Pre-Teaching the Five Words:

- *Do not* ask students if they know the meaning of the word.
- *Do not* encourage them to guess. You give them the correct meaning.
- *Do not* ask students to look up the word in the dictionary. It takes too much time, and they may select the wrong definition, especially if it is a polysemous word.
- *Do not* spend more than 1 or 2 minutes on Steps 1 to 5.
- *Do not* ask students to draw or write anything during any of these steps. Step 6 is strictly oral practice for using the word with one partner only, not the whole table.
- *Be sure* to time and allocate 1 minute to Step 6 so that students get to practice using the word *orally* with their partner at least five times each.
- *Be sure* to script out the seven steps.

In the past, most second language teaching was devoid of academic context. It took too long to teach each word. Instruction consisted mainly of isolated activities that taught basic comprehension of a simple text, if there was a text to read: flash cards, Cloze worksheets, and copying from the board. It rarely moved beyond understanding a fragment of an everyday conversation, stopping short of developing discourse capability. To move students from learning vocabulary to higher levels of oral and written discourse means a shift in ways we have been teaching. First, here are some more things to avoid to save time, effort, and disappointment.

More Things to Avoid

- Avoid using texts that limit the language too much or that contain insufficient word power and information to have meaningful discussions.
- Avoid reading to the students beyond a couple of paragraphs, even when you think a text is too difficult for students to read. When a teacher is the only one who reads, the students do not develop their vocabularies or reading comprehension skills nor delve deep into the content.
- Avoid instructional methods that take up to 20 minutes or more to teach a word. They deprive students of precious time for reading and learning more words.
- Copying definitions into word journals takes too much time. This can be a center activity later on.
- Writing sentences with the new words, before the students use them verbally with their partners in at least five examples each, does not help them remember the words and their meanings. You will need to reteach those words tomorrow all over again! This can be another center activity after reading.

Pre-teaching vocabulary should be quick, fun, and only the first time students encounter the word. This introduction is to give students the tools to put together descriptions, summaries, responses, and rich discussions around the subject they are going to read and learn. Reading will anchor language, literacy, and content knowledge.

Visual Aides

PowerPoint slides seem to be the favorite mode for presenting the seven steps. The seven steps for each word easily fits on one slide.

These can be shown on SMART Boards or with projectors. They can be easily saved on a computer for the following year. Teachers can and should use grade-level or common planning times to agree on the words to teach across the grade level or in all sections of a class. After they are taught, the words can be posted on walls under the categories of Tier 1, 2, and 3. Teachers also create table tents with lists of Tier 2 transition words, polysemous words, question starters, or sentence starters. Each table has one tent in the middle that students can view during discussions or writing activities.

REFLECT AND APPLY

What are some gradual changes you can make in your explicit instruction?

CHAPTER FIVE

Vocabulary Instruction During Reading

HOW DO STUDENTS MASTER THE WORDS?

After pre-teaching five key words, students read aloud with their partners, alternating sentences. As they read with a buddy, they begin to grasp a deeper meaning of these words in context as well as other unfamiliar words. When they finish a paragraph, they summarize orally what they learned in that paragraph, using as many Tier 2 and Tier 3 words as appear. Kindergarten and first-grade readers may need to summarize after each page or before turning the page as many emerging reader texts have one- or two-sentence paragraphs.

Students invariably have to go back and reread the paragraph and question their understanding to summarize the information correctly. This affords students a better opportunity to use the new words and acquire a better understanding of the concepts they are reading. This is also the first encounter with close reading with a purpose. The purpose is to understand the paragraph and use the vocabulary in the paragraph during reading and summarization (Nagy, 2005; Graves, August, & Carlo, 2011).

PLANNING FOR VOCABULARY MASTERY

Newly taught vocabulary must be used throughout a teaching cycle. First, a teacher selects an interesting text that addresses a content and language standard. The text ought to contain rich language to serve as a model of academic language for students—but not so difficult as to dissuade students from reading or create barriers to comprehension. Select challenging texts for ELLs but not too difficult. If they are not reading at grade level yet, try to find grade-level themes so they can keep up with the basic content concepts as they progress in language and can reach grade level quickly. Notably, ELLs begin to participate in whole-class conversations because it is a common topic where all students are using common, key Tier 3 and Tier 2 words.

Sometimes the language arts reading program calls for leveled readers where students are reading different texts. In this case, it is impossible for teachers to pre-teach text-based vocabulary, text features, and structures, much less to emulate text-based writing. One way of having all students read around a common text that facilitates ample peer interaction and depth of learning is to use common texts for science, social studies, and math. Usually, the content will be much more interesting and lead to more academic language learning. Ideally, to prevent long-term ELLs, all students should be able to start reading at grade level by the end of first grade. Vocabulary in kindergarten and first grade is a significant predictor of reading comprehension in the middle and secondary grades or of reading difficulties (Chall & Dale, 1995; Cunningham & Stanovich, 1997). When ELLs are prevented from learning and using 3,000 to 5,000 words a year, they become long-term ELLs.

The following lesson design around a common text ensures that students are using new vocabulary and learning many more words in the process of reading.

INTEGRATING VOCABULARY INTO READING AND WRITING

1. **Parse the Text.** Chunk the text into smaller sections. Common Core asks for more deliberate close reading of short, meaty texts where students can probe and ponder over words, grammatical structures, inferences, and depth of meaning. Parsing the text facilitates selecting shorter lists of words to teach. Select the words to pre-teach from each chunk. Pre-teach five or six words, and save the others for during and after reading.

2. **Teacher Highlights Content and Language Objective.** The teacher points out the math, science, social studies, or language arts learning objective as well as the vocabulary, syntax, and text structures students will encounter and be accountable for using in discussions and writing. When students understand when and how they are to master vocabulary, they will pay more attention to detail and the larger picture. They develop *semantic awareness*—they become more aware of general and domain-specific language and of prefixes, affixes, sounds, pronunciation, clauses, and sentence level features. Content and language objectives should be written in a visible location for all students and referenced before the lesson, during the lesson, and again as a reminder while explaining expectations for assignments or assessments.

3. **Teacher Think Aloud.** The teacher reads two or three sentences to model a comprehension strategy (e.g., finding cause and effect, recognizing words in context, or making inferences) while using some of the words or phrases that were pre-taught. This is also a good time to highlight text features such as graphs, subtitles, and so on. The students are instructed to listen for the comprehension strategy, repeat it to their partner, and to use it as they conduct their partner reading.

4. **Partner Reading.** Students do Partner Reading by reading aloud to each other. They read by alternating sentences in each paragraph. After each paragraph, or a page for the early grades, partners read the paragraph again to analyze the contents and summarize orally, using as many Tier 2 and 3 words as possible.

5. **More Vocabulary Instruction.** As partners read, they will encounter words that they cannot define or figure out together. Thus, they will write the word on a sticky note. As the teacher walks around monitoring the partner summaries, the sticky notes are picked up. During a pause, the teacher defines the words and gives examples, and students repeat the words and come up with examples with their buddies.

6. **Debriefing and Clarifying.** After Partner Reading, the teacher and students talk about words they encountered for

about 5 minutes. The students bring up "words they have learned" and "words not sure of." The teacher quickly clarifies misunderstandings of old and new words. It is here where you may notice the Tier 1 words some of your ELLs may not have yet (Calderón et al., 2015).

7. **Performance Assessment of Vocabulary During Reading.** Instead of the traditional vocabulary tests, plan to use a more accurate assessment of vocabulary, which is noticing and taking notes of the use of vocabulary during Step 6 (when they are using a word in their own examples) and when they are doing Partner Reading with summarization. During the observations and recording of student vocabulary practice, it is easy to note when a word is still confusing and if clarification is necessary. It also gives teachers a good perspective of how individual students are progressing and at what pace.

REFLECT AND APPLY

Thinking of your lesson plan and design, where do you plan to integrate more explicit vocabulary instruction?

CHAPTER SIX

Vocabulary Assessment and Teaching Vocabulary After Reading

More new words and phrases can be taught after reading. There are several instructional strategies that follow naturally after reading, such as students formulating questions, using cognitive maps, team presentations, a variety of cooperative learning strategies, and of course short and long pieces of writing to anchor vocabulary, discourse, and content. Learning centers or stations can also be designed for after-reading vocabulary with more words, grammar, discourse, and reading and writing activities.

SOME AFTER-READING VOCABULARY ACTIVITIES

1. **Formulating Questions.** After Partner Reading, instead of answering teacher-made questions or text questions, the students form teams of four to formulate questions from the portion of the text they have been reading using Tier 2 and Tier 3 words and phrases. Formulating instead of just answering questions develops further depth of meaning. Students need to go back into the text to do more close reading and learn more vocabulary. Using sample

question starters from Bloom's Taxonomy (see http://teaching.uncc
.edu/learning-resources/articles-books/best-practice/goals-objec
tives/writing-objectives), students in teams can jointly formulate
two questions at the Bloom level the teacher has assigned. This gives
the students additional opportunities to use the pre-taught words as
well as to learn new words as they formulate questions. It is also an
opportunity to go back into the text and delve deeper into comprehension of the topic.

2. **Assessing the Questions and the Content**. The questions
students develop are collected by the teacher, and a cooperative
learning activity can be used for the whole class to answer or discuss
the questions written by each team. This helps to anchor language,
discourse, reading comprehension, writing skills, and mastery of
content. High-quality, text-dependent questioning by students leads
to reformulation of assumptions, clarification of information, or
prediction of possible outcomes.

One strategy we used when we were conducting Multidistrict
Trainer of Trainers Institutes in each of the California Counties
of Education years ago, our presenters used a strategy to ensure
that all students were totally engaged in learning. This strategy
has been called Numbered Heads Together (Calderón, 1984;
Calderón & Spiegel-Coleman, 1985) but has been modified
throughout the years to help ELLs and SELs apply the new words
within the context of close reading and reporting what they learn
(Calderón et al., 2011–2016).

Numbered Heads Together

(1) Number off in your teams from one to four.

(2) Listen to the question.

(3) Put your heads together, and come up with the answer.

(4) Make sure every student knows the answer, particularly
your ELL peer.

(5) Be prepared if your number is called.

(6) The team that wrote the question becomes the judges of the
vocabulary used during responses.

(7) Use sentence starters, connectors, and Tier 2 and 3 words in
your response and when you add to someone else's responses.

3. **Center Activities.** Elementary teachers like to prepare activities for students to work individually or in pairs at classroom centers. It is critically important that the center activities take place after students have read, not before. At centers, students can (1) write the words, meanings, and sentences in their journals, logs, or personal dictionaries; (2) study spelling with a buddy; (3) use a computer, iPad, or tablet to practice pronunciation; (4) use a dictionary or thesaurus to further explore these words; (5) do grammar mini lessons on sentence combining, tense, or punctuation that students can use for their forthcoming drafting, revising, and editing text-based writing.

4. **Short and Long Pieces of Writing.** Initially, students write their own individual summaries or a couple of sentences on exit tickets or work on a team writing assignment. They use various strategies to revise and edit their writing before handing it in to the teacher or presenting it in class. This is the time to teach more vocabulary to students. They will need more connectors, transition words, and words for elaborating their sentences. Subsequently, they begin writing longer summaries, compositions, and reports. By now, they have used the five or six pre-taught words at least 40 times, and they own them. There is no reason to reteach any of those words. They have mastered them while reading and summarizing, formulating questions, answering questions, and doing various types of writing during all these follow-up activities.

5. **Higher-Level Discourse**. ELLs and SELs can keep up with a challenging task and pace when they experience the type of instruction described in components 1 to 7 from "Integrating Vocabulary Into Reading and Writing" in Chapter 5. They can also participate in higher-level discourse activities such as listening, repeating what proficient students are saying, and contributing with at least brief sentences. These are some of the activities in which they can participate at a modified level when provided with lists of words they can use:

(1) Oral debates or argumentative speech, where students are required to prepare background, details, positions, citations, cohesive arguments, and conclusions

(2) Oral speeches where students need to present information in a limited time frame in performances that require a beginning, middle, and end and are given cognitive maps

(3) Oral presentations of key information requiring students to know key facts and are given criteria and rubrics to read the audience, protocols to be aware of time and tone, and specific relevant vocabulary to use

(4) Oral interviews for jobs, scholarships, internships, or other situations, where students need to convince the audience of their skills and potential

(5) Sales and marketing advertising, where students need to sell both the merits of a product or service and their personal expertise with and knowledge of it

(6) Understanding, acknowledging, or presenting various points of view; for example, during a crime investigation, a student may be asked to play a police officer, attorney, clergy, witness, teacher, counselor, TV reporter, parent, friend, or other stakeholder.

(7) Oral variations and vocabulary needed for representing a specific profession in a technical or professional manner, such as a theater actor, a poet, a police officer, a painter, an architect, an athlete, a scientist, or a university professor (adapted from CCSS).

Assessing Vocabulary Mastery

There are several steps along the lesson path to assess the progress and mastery of vocabulary.

First, the objectives and expectations need to be set in a way that one can return and assess what has been accomplished. For example, after students read a book such as *I Can Stay Calm* or *Don't Give Up* and the vocabulary includes words such as *resiliency*, the objectives can be as follows:

Content Objectives—Use evidence from the text to do the following:

- Identify statements about resiliency made by the author.
- Determine and explain what evidence the author used to support these statements or claims.
- Determine the connections to our lives.
- Describe cause-and-effect relationships explained by the author.

Language Objectives—Acquire and use new vocabulary sufficient for reading, writing, speaking, and listening.

- Reading: Determine main idea and provide summary of the text using Tier 2 and Tier 3 words. Identify and justify the claims made by the author.
- Listening and Speaking: Engage effectively in a range of collaborative discussions.
- Writing: Develop and strengthen writing by collaborating in drafting, revising, editing, rewriting, and sharing a final product.

Second, the assessments occur during the listening, speaking, reading, and writing events. The assessments can take several forms:

(1) Scripting individual performance and keeping those narratives in the student's folders or portfolios

(2) Using a checklist (meets expectation, in progress, or not performed) that looks at how many and how well Tier 2 and Tier 3 words are being used in the following activities:

   (a) Vocabulary Step 6 (five adequate examples of each word taught)

   (b) Partner Reading verbal summaries after each paragraph

   (c) Words and sentences in exit or entry passes or tickets

   (d) Question formulation and question responses during Numbered Heads Together

   (e) Class discussions on *resiliency*

   (f) Cooperative learning discourse activities using former and current vocabulary

   (g) Collaborative writing that includes the teacher's criteria for assessing the writing in addition to the appropriate use of connectors, transition words, and new vocabulary—the criteria must be as explicit as possible; for instance, the writer must accomplish the following:

      - Establish a context, introduce a narrator or characters, and organize an event sequence.

- Employ narrative techniques such as dialogue, description to develop experiences, events, and/or characters.
- Use a variety of transition words to convey sequence and signal shifts.
- Use precise words and phrases, relevant descriptive details, and sensory language.
- Provide a conclusion that follows from and reflects on the narrated experiences or events.

Third, inform the students how you will measure each—how many points per each criteria met.

Fourth, use a grid to keep on hand as a reminder. The two tables that follow are examples of ways teachers plan their assessments.

Learning Objectives	ExC-ELL Observation Protocol™ (EOP®) Assessment Checklist
Listening and Speaking: Engage in a variety of collaborative discussions with diverse partners based on a common text. Build on others' ideas, and express one's own ideas clearly in complete sentences.	Listening and Speaking: Use teacher documentation of oral summaries during partner reading, question formulation, and responses during Numbered Heads Together.
Writing: Write a narrative to develop imagined experiences or events using descriptive details, dialogue, and clear event sequences.	Writing: Use data from daily or weekly exit passes, written summaries, and independent writing. Note: Use story and paragraph frames or other aids to differentiate for students who need support.

Summary

Vocabulary is to be integrated throughout a lesson. Some words and phrases can be taught before (1) students read, (2) listen to a teacher's presentation of content, (3) observe and listen to an experiment, (4) watch a video, or (5) listen to a teacher read a storybook aloud to them —so that the students are not totally lost. Yet, the most effective way to master those words is through repetitive almost redundant use during reading, discussions, and writing.

The Common Core State Standards call for delving deeply into word knowledge in the process of close reading and text-based writing. Hence, vocabulary should be selected from the texts students are about to read and reinforced through reading them in context, using the words as they read to summarize verbally, answer and formulate questions, and compose different types of writing in all the subject areas. The way we speak, read, and write in language arts is very different from the way we do that in math, science, social studies, and several other subjects. When ELLs and SELs in elementary schools learn how to use 3,000 to 5,000 words per year in all subjects combined, secondary schools will not experience so many long-term ELLs. When ELLs and SELs master at least five words per subject per day in their secondary schools, they will be career and college ready. Hence, it behooves all educators in a school to embrace vocabulary instruction as a critical foundation for all content areas.

CHAPTER SEVEN

Conclusions, Challenges, and Connections

This book began by connecting the research on academic language and literacy to academic vocabulary, with particular emphasis on Tier 2 and Tier 3 academic words. A system for selecting words to teach, a seven-step process for pre-teaching vocabulary, and methods for teaching vocabulary during and after instruction were also introduced.

OVERCOMING CHALLENGES

As discussed in Chapter 1, some teachers may feel overwhelmed when trying to determine and meet the vast vocabulary needs of their ELLs and SELs. Pre-assessing word knowledge for a class may be a helpful place to determine specific vocabulary needs. For this process, both Tier 2 and Tier 3 words from a unit or reading selection can be chosen, and students can be asked to rank their prior knowledge of a word (Soto-Hinman & Hetzel, 2009). The pre-assessments can then be reviewed for the class, and the Tier 2 and Tier 3 words that students struggle with most can be taught explicitly, using the strategies recommended in this book in the series.

Another vocabulary challenge for educators might be the vast variety of vocabulary needs within the classroom. Some students may have prior knowledge of Tier 2 and Tier 3 words, whereas others, including ELLs and SELs, may not. Intentional pairing of students can assist with this gap so that the teacher does not become the only language model in the room. When ELLs or SELs are paired with a linguistic model, they can use the language or vocabulary that was modeled for them in their own spoken or written language, which might be more language than they had on their own. Appropriate and intentional pairing of students, then, becomes a resource for everyone in the room.

TUNING PROTOCOL: POWERFUL PROFESSIONAL LEARNING TO ENHANCE ELL AND SEL ACHIEVEMENT

To understand and implement the work of this series, we advocate sustained, job-embedded professional learning that is grounded in the work of teacher teams. Reading this book can be a starting place for such learning, and the Tuning Protocol is a tool for self-reflection when analyzing student work samples for ALD.

Specifically, the Tuning Protocol is a powerful design for professional learning that is based on collaborative analysis of student work. Due to the fact that it takes focused professional development over time to change major instructional practices, we recommend that a recursive professional development sequence, like the Tuning Protocol, be used along with the book series. The Tuning Protocol, developed by the Coalition of Essential Schools (Blythe, Allen, & Powell, 1999), can be effective as a way to more deeply explore ALD strategies and approaches recommended throughout the book series. For example, a department or grade level may choose to analyze student work samples from ELLs and/or SELs that address paragraph structures from *Grammar and Syntax in Context* or to analyze the conversational skill of clarifying ideas from *Conversational Discourse in Context*. A full-cycle collaborative conversation of the Tuning Protocol for culturally responsive teaching is provided here, and the process is also included in the epilogue.

THE TUNING PROTOCOL

(1) Presenter describes context of work to be analyzed (e.g., student level, curriculum, or time allotted).

Presenter determines focus question, which will be the lens by which the work will be analyzed.

(2) Group silently reviews work and asks clarifying questions only (e.g., How long did it take?).

(3) Group takes notes on warm and cool feedback *regarding the focus question only*.

(4) Group shares warm and cool feedback.

(5) Presenter reflects on next steps for instruction

(Adapted from Soto, 2012)

TUNING PROTOCOL FOR THE SEVEN-STEP PROCESS FOR PRE-TEACHING VOCABULARY

In Chapter 6, you read about how to assess vocabulary via short and long pieces of writing. This process is described in this volume:

> Initially, students write their own individual summaries or a couple of sentences on exit tickets or work on a team writing assignment. They use various strategies to revise and edit their writing before handing it in to the teacher or presenting it in class. This is the time to teach more vocabulary to students. They will need more connectors, transition words, and words for elaborating their sentences. Subsequently, they begin writing longer summaries, compositions, and reports. By now, they have used the five or six pre-taught words at least 40 times, and they own them.

Once students have written their short or long pieces of writing, incorporating the key vocabulary previously taught, a group of teachers analyzes an individual ELL or SEL writing sample on the incorporation of key vocabulary in the writing using the five-step Tuning Protocol, as follows:

(1) **Teacher describes the context of the work to the group**— "I pre-taught key vocabulary from the story *Stellaluna* (the story of a bat who is separated from her mother and raised by birds). I used the seven-step process for pre-teaching vocabulary for each of the key vocabulary that I then required students to use in their summary of the text."

   (a) **Presenter determines focus question for analysis of student sample**—The teacher decides that as her colleagues analyze the student work sample for the incorporation of key vocabulary, she would like feedback on how well her students were able to apply those words in their own writing. The focus question then becomes: "How can I assist my ELLs with incorporating key vocabulary into their own writing?"

(2) **Group reviews work and asks clarifying questions**—One colleague asked the clarifying question: "How long did it take you to first introduce the seven-step process for pre-teaching vocabulary?" The teacher responds, "It took me longer the first time that I used the process, but after a while, students got used to it, so it went much faster. I used PowerPoint slides to introduce each step and kept them up for reference points, and then I also modeled each step with a student I had prepared in front of the class."

   (b) **Group individually takes notes, highlighting warm and cool feedback**—For warm feedback, participants will analyze the student work sample for everything that was done well, from punctuation to subject-verb agreement, to penmanship. For cool (not cold) feedback, participants will analyze the student work sample only for incorporation of the key vocabulary. Recall that the teacher presenter selected the focus question so that he or she is in control of the type of cool feedback that he or she would like to receive. In this example, the teacher asked for the following cool feedback: "How can I assist my ELLs with incorporating key vocabulary into their own writing?"

(c) **Group shares warm and cool feedback**—One at a time, participants in the group share warm feedback first. It is helpful to use objective frames when providing feedback, such as "I noticed (*for observations*)" and "I wonder (*for questions*)." It is also important to begin with warm feedback, as we all want to be viewed from an asset model first. A sample warm feedback statement might be: "*I noticed* that the student incorporated most of the key vocabulary into their writing." (Please note that if the Tuning Protocol is being used with a large group, the group facilitator will want to select a few warm and cool feedback statements.) Once the warm feedback has been shared, cool feedback statements can be provided. Recall that cool feedback is based on the focus question only. In this case, the teacher wanted cool feedback regarding the following question: "How can I assist my ELLs with incorporating key vocabulary into their own writing?" A sample cool feedback statement might be: "Although the student incorporated most of the key vocabulary into their writing, I *wonder* if he or she might incorporate all of them, if the student had the introductory PowerPoint in front of him or her as a reminder."

(3) **Presenter reflects on feedback provided**—after all of the warm and cool feedback has been provided, the teacher presenter reflects on his or her next steps from the group discussion of the student work sample on supporting ideas. A sample reflective statement might be: "My next step with ensuring that all key vocabulary is transferred into student writing is to have all of the words posted and/or listed on the PowerPoint when students begin to write. I might also quickly review the PowerPoint before they begin writing."

We recognize that for many teachers, the ideas in this book and the book series will require time and practice. Both sustained professional development over time (which can include the Tuning Protocol) and instructional coaching can be helpful tools. It is also important for educators to remember to go slow to go fast, that is, to realize that the strategies and instructional approaches outlined will take time to approximate. In this manner, just as we honor the assets of our children, let's honor the assets of our teachers as excellent learners, who can take on new challenges with appropriate and sustained professional development over time.

ALD BOOK SERIES SUMMARY
AND INTERSECTIONS ACROSS THE BOOKS

As suggested earlier, the purpose of this four-book series is to assist educators in developing expertise in, and practical strategies for, addressing the key dimensions of academic language when working with ELLs and SELs. In order to systemically address the needs of ELLs and SELs, we educators must share a common understanding of academic language development and the interconnectedness of its four dimensions.

The following chart provides a summary of the ALD dimension, as well as intersections across the book series. To truly create systemic change for ELLs and SELs in the area of ALD, there must be a deep understanding of each of the dimensions of ALD under study, as well as sustained professional development and instructional efforts to address each dimension, which will be addressed throughout the book series. The book series summary can assist the reader with where to begin when reading the series, and the intersections across the book series can assist with making connections as one completes each book.

This chart allows us to better understand how ALD can and will support ELLs and SELs to make connections within new rigorous standards and expectations. Meaningful and intentional planning around each ALD dimension will allow access for ELLs and SELs into content that might otherwise be inaccessible to them. In the epilogue, you will learn how to use this series in professional development settings and how the book series connects to culturally and linguistically responsive practices.

ALD Dimension	Book Series Summary	Intersections Across Book Series

Conversational Discourse	Zwiers (2016) defines *conversational discourse* as the use of language for extended, back-and-forth, and purposeful communication among people. A key feature of conversational discourse is that it is used to create and clarify knowledge, not just transmit it.
	
	The essential skills of conversational discourse include the following:
	
	    • Conversing with a purpose
	    • Clarifying ideas
	    • Supporting ideas and finding evidence
	    • Evaluating evidence and reasoning
	    • Negotiating ideas
	
	Successful conversational discourse for ELLs and SELs requires a safe classroom culture and appropriate scaffolds for conversation.
		• Conversational discourse necessarily connects to the development of *academic vocabulary* and to its written counterpart, academic writing across genres.
		• It connects to *grammar and syntax in context* through the need to make and express meaning at the text, paragraph, and sentence levels.
		• It connects to *culturally and linguistically responsive practices* by engaging students in cooperative practices and respectful listening to other points of view and backgrounds.

Academic Vocabulary	This volume defines *academic vocabulary* as a combination of words, phrases, sentences, and strategies to participate in class discussions, to show evidence of understanding and express complex concepts in texts, and to express oneself in academic writing.	• Academic vocabulary, according to Calderón, is the centerpiece of *conversational discourse.* • It connects to *grammar and syntax in context* naturally in that vocabulary is also taught within context. The two dimensions mutually provide meaning for one another.

(Continued)

(Continued)

ALD Dimension	Book Series Summary	Intersections Across Book Series
(Academic Vocabulary)	To enhance academic vocabulary for ELLs and SELs, teachers select words to specifically teach before, during, and after instruction. They select words and phrases that they believe ELLs and SELs need: • to know to comprehend the text • to discuss those concepts • to use in their writing later on	• It connects to *culturally and linguistically responsive practices* in making understandable the distinctions between some common misuses of words ("berry" instead of "very") and the standard English word association.
Grammar and Syntax in Context	According to Soto, Freeman, and Freeman (2016), academic texts pose a particular challenge to ELLs and SELs because they contain technical vocabulary and grammatical structures that are lexically dense and abstract. These include long nominal groups, passives, and complex sentences. ELLs and SELs need carefully scaffolded instruction to write the academic genres, make the writing cohesive, and use appropriate grammatical structures.	• ELLs and SELs need to be engaged in academic discourse to develop their oral academic language. This provides the base for reading and writing academic texts. • ELLs and SELs also need to develop academic vocabulary, both content specific vocabulary and general academic vocabulary that they can use as they read and write the academic genres. Teachers should use culturally and linguistically responsive practices that enable students to draw on their full linguistic repertoires.

ALD Dimension	Book Series Summary	Intersections Across Book Series
Culturally and Linguistically Responsive Practices	LeMoine cites Gay (2000) in *defining culturally and linguistically responsive practices* as "ways of knowing, understanding, and representing various ethnic groups in teaching academic subjects, processes, and skills." Its primary features benefitting ELLs and SELs include the following: • Promoting cooperation, collaboration, reciprocity, and mutual responsibility for learning • Incorporating high-status, accurate cultural knowledge about different groups of students • Cultivating the cultural integrity, individual abilities, and academic success of diverse student groups. Simply stated, it is meaningful learning embedded in language and culture.	• Culturally and linguistically responsive practices connect to the development of *academic vocabulary* by providing recognition for prior knowledge and acknowledging culture as part of linguistic development. • It connects to *conversational discourse* by prioritizing cooperative conversation procedures and minimizing confrontational discourse. • It connects to *grammar and syntax in context* by building on second language acquisition strategies and methods (such as SDAIE [Specially Designed Academic Instruction in English] and contrastive analysis).

Epilogue: The Vision

The vision for this book series began with the formation of the Institute for Culturally and Linguistically Responsive Teaching (ICLRT) at Whittier College, the creation of the ICLRT Design Principles, which guides the institute, and the development of an ALD book series, which can assist educators with more deeply meeting the needs of their ELLs and SELs. ICLRT was formed in 2014, and the institute's mission is to "promote relevant research and develop academic resources for ELLs and Standard English Learners (SELs) via linguistically and culturally responsive teaching practices" (ICLRT, n.d.). As such, ICLRT's purpose is to "Provide research-based and practitioner-oriented professional development services, tools, and resources for K–12 systems and teacher education programs serving ELLs and SELs." Whittier College is a nationally designated Hispanic-Serving Institution, and ICLRT staff have been providing professional development on ELLs and SELs for more than 15 years, both across California and nationally.

The four books in this ALD series build upon the foundation of the ICLRT Design Principles:

(1) Connecting and addressing the needs of both ELLs and SELs, both linguistically and culturally

(2) Assisting educators with identifying ways to use this book series (and additional ICLRT books) in professional development settings

(3) Addressing the underdeveloped domains of speaking and listening as areas that can be integrated across disciplines and components of ALD

(4) Integrating culturally responsive teaching as a vehicle for honoring both home and primary languages, as well as cultural norms for learning

ICLRT Design Principles

Here is a complete list of the ICLRT Design Principles. In parentheses are the books in this series that will address each principle.

(1) **ICLRT believes that the commonalities between ELL and SEL students are more extensive (and more vital to their learning) than the differences between the two groups.**

- ELL and SEL students are at the same end of the learning gap – they often score at the lowest levels on achievement tests. They also rank highly among high school dropouts (*Culture in Context*).
- The academic progress of ELL and SEL students may be hindered by barriers, such as poor identification practices and negative teacher attitudes toward their languages and cultures (*Culture in Context*).
- ELL and SEL students both need specific instructional attention to the development of academic language development (*Grammar and Syntax in Context*, *Conversational Discourse*, and *Vocabulary in Context*).

(2) **ICLRT believes that ongoing, targeted professional development is the key to redirecting teacher attitudes toward ELL and SEL student groups.**

- Teacher knowledge about the histories and cultures of ELL and SEL students can be addressed through professional development and professional learning communities (*Culture in Context*).
- Teachers will become aware of the origins of nonstandard language usage (*Culture in Context*).
- Teachers can become aware of and comfortable with using diverse texts and productive group work to enhance student sense of belonging (*Conversational Discourse in Context*).

- The ICLRT Academic Language Certification process will provide local demonstration models of appropriate practices and attitudes (*Conversational Discourse in Context*).

(3) **ICLRT believes that ELL and SEL students need to have ongoing, progressive opportunities for listening and speaking throughout their school experiences.**

- The typical ELD sequence of curriculum and courses does not substantially address ELL and SEL student needs for language development (*Conversational Discourse in Context* and *Vocabulary in Context*).
- The ICLRT student shadowing protocol and student shadowing app can provide both quantitative and qualitative information about student speaking and listening (*Conversational Discourse in Context*).
- The ICLRT lesson plan design incorporates appropriate speaking and listening development integrated with reading, writing, and/or content area learning (*Conversational Discourse in Context*).
- Strategies for active listening and academic oral language are embedded in ICLRT's ALD professional development series (*Conversational Discourse in Context*).

(4) **ICLRT believes that its blending of culturally responsive pedagogy (CRP) with ALD will provide teachers of ELL and SEL students with powerful learning tools and strategies.**

- The six characteristics of CRP (Gay, 2000), along with the procedure of contrastive analysis, heighten the already strong effects of solid ALD instruction (*Grammar and Syntax in Context*).
- The storytelling aspects of CRP fit well with the oral language traditions of ELLs and can be used as a foundational tool for both groups to affirm their rich histories (*Culture in Context*).
- Both groups need specific instruction in the four essential components of ALD, including SDAIE strategies (*Grammar and Syntax in Context, Conversational Discourse*, and *Vocabulary in Context*).

- The inclusion of CRP and ALD within the ICLRT lesson planning tool makes their use seamless, instead of disparate for each group (*Culture in Context*).

Sources: Gay, 2000; LeMoine, 1999; Soto-Hinman & Hetzel, 2009.

Additional ICLRT Professional Development Resources

This ALD book series is one of the research-based resources developed by ICLRT to assist K–12 systems in serving ELLs and SELs. Other ICLRT resources include the following Corwin texts: *The Literacy Gaps: Building Bridges for ELLs and SELs* (Soto-Hinman & Hetzel, 2009); *ELL Shadowing as a Catalyst for Change* (Soto, 2012); and *Moving From Spoken to Written Language With ELLs* (Soto, 2014). Together, the three books, and their respective professional development modules (available via ICLRT and Corwin), tell a story of how to systemically close achievement gaps with ELLs and SELs by increasing their academic oral language production in academic areas. Specifically, each ICLRT book in the series addresses ALD in the following ways.

- *The Literacy Gaps: Building Bridges for ELLs and SELs* (Soto-Hinman & Hetzel, 2009)—This book is a primer for meeting the literacy needs of ELLs and SELs. Additionally, the linguistic and achievement needs of ELLs and SELs are linked and specific ALD strategies are outlined to comprehensively and coherently meet the needs of both groups of students.
- *ELL Shadowing as a Catalyst for Change* (Soto, 2012)—This book is a way to create urgency around meeting the academic oral language needs of ELLs. Educators shadow an ELL student, guided by the ELL shadowing protocol, which allows them to monitor and collect academic oral language and active listening data. The ethnographic project allows educators to experience a day in the life of an ELL.
- *Moving From Spoken to Written Language With ELLs* (Soto, 2014)—This book assists educators in leveraging spoken language into written language. Specific strategies, such as Think-Pair-Share, the Frayer model, and Reciprocal

Teaching, are used to scaffold the writing process, and the Curriculum Cycle (Gibbons, 2002) is recommended as a framework for teaching writing.

Please note that professional development modules for each of the texts listed are also available through ICLRT. For more information, please go to www.whittier.edu/ICLRT.

The ALD book series can be used either after or alongside of *The Literacy Gaps: Building Bridges for ELLs and SELs* (Soto-Hinman & Hetzel, 2009); *ELL Shadowing as a Catalyst for Change* (Soto, 2012); and *Moving From Spoken to Written Language With ELLs* (Soto, 2014) as each book introduces and addresses the importance of ALD for ELLs and SELs. The ALD book series also takes each ALD component deeper by presenting specific research and strategies that will benefit ELLs and SELs in the classroom.

References

Academic Language Development Network. (n.d.). Retrieved from http://aldnetwork.org/

Biemiller, A. (2011). Vocabulary: What words should we teach? *Better: Evidence-Based Education*, *3(2)*, 10–11. Baltimore, MD: Johns Hopkins University. Retrieved from http://www.betterevidence.org/uk-edition/issue-6/vocabulary-what-words-should-we-teach/

Beck, I. L., McKeown, M. G., & Kucan, L. (2002). *Bringing words to life.* New York: Guilford.

Beck, I. L., McKeown, M. G., & Kucan, L. (2005). Choosing words to teach. In E. H. Hiebert & M. L. Kamil (Eds.), *Teaching and learning vocabulary* (pp. 207–222). Mahwah, NJ: Lawrence Erlbaum.

Blythe, T., Allen, D., & Powell, B. S. (1999). *Looking together at student work.* New York: College Teachers Press.

Calderón, M. (1984). *Sheltered instruction: Manual for teachers and teacher trainers.* San Diego, CA: Multifunctional Resource Center.

Calderón, M. E. (2007). *Teaching reading to English language learners, Grades 6-12: A framework for improving achievement in the content areas.* Thousand Oaks, CA: Corwin.

Calderón, M. E. (2011). *Teaching reading and comprehension to English learners, K–5.* Indianapolis, IN: Solution Tree.

Calderón, M., August, D., Slavin, R., Cheung, A., Durán, D., & Madden, N. (2005). Bringing words to life in classrooms with English language learners. In A. Hiebert & M. Kamil (Eds.), *Research and development on vocabulary.* Mahwah, NJ: Lawrence Erlbaum.

Calderón, M., Carreón, A., Duran, D., & Fitch, A. (2009). *Preparing math, science, social studies and language arts teachers with English learners: Report to the Carnegie Corporation of New York.* New York: The Carnegie Corporation of New York.

Calderón, M. E., Carreón, A., Slakk, S., Trejo, M., & Peyton, J. (2010–2016). *Expediting comprehension for English language learners (ExC-ELL) foundations manual.* New Rochelle, NY: Benchmark Education.

Calderón, M. E., & Slakk, S. S. (in press). *Teaching vocabulary.* Indianapolis, IN: Solution Tree.

Calderón, M., & Spiegel-Coleman, S. (1985). Effective instruction for language minority students—from theory to practice. *Teacher Education Journal, 2*(3).

Calderón, M. E., Trejo, M., Montenegro, H., Carreón, A. Peyton, J. K., Marino, J., & D'Emilio, T. (2015). *Literacy strategies for English learners in core content secondary classrooms.* Indianapolis, IN: Solution Tree.

California State Board of Education. (2013). *California Common Core State Standards English language arts & literacy in history/social studies, science, and technical subjects.* Sacramento: Author. Retrieved from http://www.cde.ca.gov/re/pn/rc

Campbell, G. M. (1994). Transition words. Retrieved from https://msu .edu/~jdowell/135/transw.html

Chall, J., & Dale, E. (1995). *Readability revisited.* Cambridge, MA: Brookline.

Crawford-Brooke, E. (2013). *The critical role of oral language in reading for Title I students and English language learners.* Lexia Learning. Retrieved from http://lexialearning.com/lexiaresearch/whitepapers/ oral-language-whitepaper

Cunningham, A. E., & Stanovich, K. E. (1997). Early reading acquisition and its relation to reading experience and ability 10 years later. *Developmental Psychology, 33*(6), 934–945.

Gay, G. (2000). *Culturally responsive teaching: Theory, research, and practice.* New York: Teachers College Press.

Gibbons, P. (2002). *Scaffolding language, scaffolding learning: Teaching second language learners in the mainstream classroom.* Portsmouth, NH: Heinemann.

Graves, M. F. (2006). *The vocabulary book: Learning and instruction.* New York: Teachers College Press.

Graves, M., August, D., & Carlo, M. (2011, Winter). Teaching 50,000 words. *Better: Evidence-Based Education, 3*(2), 6–7. Retrieved from http://esl.ncwiseowl.org/UserFiles/Servers/Server_4502383/File/all.pdf

Hadley, A. O. (1993). *Teaching language in context.* Boston: Heinle & Heinle.

Hiebert, E. H., & Kamil, M. L. (2005). *Teaching and learning vocabulary: Bringing research to practice.* Mahwah, NJ: Lawrence Erlbaum.

Institute for Culturally and Linguistically Responsive Teaching (ICLRT). (n.d.). Retrieved from http://www.whittier.edu/ICLRT

LeMoine, N., & L. A. Unified School District. (1999). *English for your success: A language development program for African American students. Handbook of successful strategies for educators.* NJ: The Peoples Publishing Group.

Migration Policy Institute Tabulation of Data From the United Nations, Department of Economic and Social Affairs. (2013). Trends in international migrant stock: Migrants by origin and destination, 2013 revision (United Nations database, POP/DB/MIG/Stock/Rev.2013). Retrieved from http://esa.un.org/unmigration/TIMSO2013/migrantstocks2013.htm

Nagy, W. (2005). Why vocabulary instruction needs to be long-term and comprehensive. In E. H. Hiebert & M. L. Kamil (Eds.), *Teaching and learning vocabulary. Bringing research to practice* (pp. 27–44). Mahwah, NJ: Lawrence Erlbaum.

National Governors Association Center for Best Practices, & Council of Chief State School Officers. (2010). Common Core State Standards for English language arts & literacy in history/social studies, science, and technical subjects. Washington, DC: Authors.

Peyton, J. (2014). *Human migration and global change.* Washington, DC. Margarita Calderón & Associates Publications.

Short, D. J., & Fitzsimmons, S. (2007). *Double the work: Challenges and solutions to acquiring language and academic literacy for adolescent English language learners.* Washington, DC: Alliance for Excellent Education.

Slavin, R. E., Madden, N. A., Calderón, M. E., Chamberlain, A., & Hennessy, M. (2011). Reading and language outcomes of a five-year randomized evaluation of transitional bilingual education. *Educational Evaluation and Policy Analysis, 33*(1), 47–58. Retrieved from http://www.edweek.org/media/bilingual_pdf.pdf

Soto, I. (2012). *ELL shadowing as a catalyst for change.* Thousand Oaks, CA: Corwin.

Soto, I. (2014). *From spoken to written language with ELLs.* Thousand Oaks, CA: Corwin.

Soto, I., Freeman, D., & Freeman, Y. (2016). *Academic English mastery: Grammar and syntax in context.* Thousand Oaks, CA: Corwin.

Soto, G., & S. Guevara (1995). *Chato's kitchen.* New York: G. P. Putnam's Sons.

Soto-Hinman, I., & Hetzel, J. (2009). *The literacy gaps: Building bridges for ELLs and SELs.* Thousand Oaks, CA: Corwin.

Wong-Fillmore, L. (2013). Defining academic language. *Education Week.* Retrieved from http://www.edweek.org/ew/articles/2013/10/30/10cc-academiclanguage.h33.html

Zwiers, J. (2016). *Academic English mastery: Conversational skills in context.* Thousand Oaks, CA: Corwin.

Index

IS YOUR ACADEMIC LANGUAGE MASTERY LIBRARY COMPLETE?

Academic Language Mastery: Conversational Discourse in Context
Jeff Zwiers and Ivannia Soto

Here, Jeff Zwiers reveals the power of academic conversation in helping students develop language, clarify concepts, comprehend complex texts, and fortify thinking and relational skills. With this book as your road map, you'll learn how to

- Foster the skills and language students must develop for productive interactions
- Implement strategies for scaffolding conversations between students
- Formatively assess students' oral language development

Academic Language Mastery: Grammar and Syntax in Context
David E. Freeman, Yvonne S. Freeman, and Ivannia Soto

David and Yvonne Freeman shatter the myth that academic language is all about vocabulary, revealing how grammar and syntax inform ELLs' and SELs' grasp of challenging text. Inside you'll find research-backed advice on how to

- Teach grammar in the context of students' speech and writing
- Use strategies such as sentence frames, passives, combining simple sentences into more complex sentences, and nominalization to create more complex noun phrases
- Assess academic language development through a four-step process

Academic Language Mastery: Culture in Context
Noma LeMoine and Ivannia Soto

Never underestimate the critical role culture and language play in our students' education. In this volume, Noma LeMoine offers new insight on how culturally and linguistically responsive pedagogy validates, facilitates, liberates, and empowers our diverse students. Learn how to

- Implement instructional strategies designed to meet the linguistic and cultural needs of ELLs and SELs
- Use language variation as an asset in the classroom
- Recognize and honor prior knowledge, home languages, and cultures

For more information, visit www.corwin.com!

A SAGE Publishing Company

Helping educators make the greatest impact

CORWIN HAS ONE MISSION: to enhance education through intentional professional learning.

We build long-term relationships with our authors, educators, clients, and associations who partner with us to develop and continuously improve the best evidence-based practices that establish and support lifelong learning.

Solutions you want. Experts you trust. Results you need.

AUTHOR CONSULTING

Author Consulting

On-site professional learning with sustainable results! Let us help you design a professional learning plan to meet the unique needs of your school or district. www.corwin.com/pd

INSTITUTES

Institutes

Corwin Institutes provide collaborative learning experiences that equip your team with tools and action plans ready for immediate implementation. www.corwin.com/institutes

ECOURSES

eCourses

Practical, flexible online professional learning designed to let you go at your own pace. www.corwin.com/ecourses

READ2EARN

Read2Earn

Did you know you can earn graduate credit for reading this book? Find out how: www.corwin.com/read2earn

Contact an account manager at (800) 831-6640 or visit **www.corwin.com** for more information.